Software Process Improvement

Software Process Improvement

Zico Pratama Putra

SADIN
PRESS

2025

First Printing: 2025

ISBN-13: 9798281859158

Sadin Press
Jl. Raya Centex
Jakarta, Indonesia

Bookstores and wholesalers: Please contact Sadin Press email

zico.zpp@nusamandiri.ac.id.

Trademark Acknowledgments

Product or corporate names mentioned in this book may be the trademarks or registered trademarks of their respective owners.

Unless otherwise indicated herein, any the third-party trademarks that may appear in this work are the property of their respective owners and any references to the third-party trademark, logos or other trade dress are for demonstrative or descriptive purposes only

Ordering Information: Special discounts are available on quantity purchases by corporations, associations, educators, and others. For details, contact the publisher at the above-listed address.

PREFACE

Welcome to the Software Process Improvement. This book has been meticulously crafted to serve as a comprehensive resource for university students and professionals seeking to deepen their understanding of software process improvement and quality management. It is designed to bridge the gap between theoretical knowledge and practical application, providing readers with a solid foundation in the principles and practices that drive successful software development.

Purpose of the Book

The primary goal of this book is to equip readers with the knowledge and tools necessary to navigate the complex landscape of software engineering. In today's fast-paced technological environment, the demand for high-quality software solutions is ever-increasing. This book aims to address this demand by providing a thorough exploration of the methodologies, frameworks, and best practices that have proven effective in the industry.

Intended Audience

This book is intended for a diverse audience, including undergraduate and graduate students in computer science, software engineering, and related fields. It is also a valuable resource for professionals who are looking to enhance their skills in software process improvement and quality management. Whether you are a student embarking on your first software project or a seasoned developer seeking to refine your practices, this book offers insights that will be beneficial throughout your career.

How to Use the Book

The book is structured to be both modular and progressive. Each chapter builds upon the concepts introduced in the previous ones, allowing readers to follow a logical learning path. However, the modular design also means that readers can easily navigate to specific topics of interest without needing to read the entire book sequentially.

- **For Students**: Use this book as a companion to your coursework. Each chapter includes exercises and questions designed to reinforce key concepts and encourage critical thinking. The real-world examples and case studies will help you see how these principles are applied in practice.

- **For Professionals**: This book serves as a reference guide that you can consult as needed. The detailed explanations and practical advice will help you address challenges in your current projects and stay updated with the latest trends and best practices.

Structure of the Book

The book is divided into several chapters, each focusing on a specific aspect of software process improvement and quality management. From an introduction to the strategic role of software quality to in-depth explorations of process models, quality management systems, and risk management, the content is designed to provide a holistic view of the field.

Chapter 1 introduces the fundamental concepts of software process improvement and the strategic importance of software quality.

Chapter 2 delves into various software process models, including the Waterfall, Evolutionary Development, Component-based Software Engineering, Incremental, and Spiral models.

Chapter 3 explores the principles of software quality management, including quality assurance, quality control, and the ISO 9000 standards.

Chapter 4 examines process improvement frameworks such as CMMI, Six Sigma, and Lean Six Sigma.

Chapter 5 discusses process analysis and measurement techniques, including the Goal Question Metric Paradigm.

Chapter 6 focuses on software testing strategies, including verification and validation, levels of testing, and testing techniques.

Chapter 7 covers data reporting and analysis, with a focus on qualitative data analysis and grounded theory.

Chapter 8 provides an overview of systems development methodologies, including the traditional SDLC and alternative approaches like Prototyping and Rapid Application Development.

Chapter 9 addresses risk management and decision-making in software projects.

Chapter 10 introduces the eSourcing Capability Model (eSCM) for both service providers and client organizations.

Chapter 11 explores the IT Infrastructure Library (ITIL) and its role in IT service management.

Chapter 12 examines ISO standards and models relevant to software engineering.

Chapter 13 presents real-world case studies and practical applications of the concepts discussed.

Chapter 14 looks at future trends and challenges in software process improvement and quality management.

Additional Resources

To enhance your learning experience, the book includes appendices with glossaries, sample templates, and additional resources. These supplementary materials are designed to provide practical tools and references that you can use in your studies or professional practice.

Acknowledgments

I would like to express my sincere gratitude to all those who have contributed to the development of this book. Special thanks to my colleagues and students, whose insights and experiences have greatly enriched the content. I am also grateful to the team at Moonshot AI for their support and assistance in bringing this project to fruition.

Certainly! Below is a draft introduction for your book based on the framework provided and the content of your lecture slides.

INTRODUCTION TO THE BOOK

Welcome to the Software Process Improvement. This book is designed to provide a thorough and practical understanding of the principles and practices that drive successful software development. Whether you are a student embarking on your first software project or a seasoned professional looking to refine your skills, this book aims to be a valuable resource.

The Importance of Software Process Improvement

In today's rapidly evolving technological landscape, the demand for high-quality software solutions is ever-increasing. Software process improvement is not just a buzzword; it is a critical practice that ensures software projects are delivered on time, within budget, and with the desired quality. Effective software processes help organizations manage complexity, reduce risks, and enhance productivity. They also play a crucial role in fostering innovation and maintaining a competitive edge in the market.

Strategic Role of Software Quality

Software quality is a cornerstone of successful software development. It encompasses not only the functionality and reliability of the software but also its maintainability, usability, and scalability. High-quality software meets user expectations, performs efficiently, and can be easily adapted to changing requirements. This book emphasizes the strategic importance of software quality and explores how it can be achieved through rigorous process improvement and management.

Continuous Improvement

The journey towards software process improvement is a continuous one. It involves ongoing assessment, adaptation, and enhancement of existing processes. This book provides a comprehensive overview of the methodologies, frameworks, and best practices that have proven effective in the industry. From traditional process models like the Waterfall and Incremental models to modern approaches like Agile and Lean, we will explore a variety of strategies that can be tailored to meet the specific needs of different projects and organizations.

Process Models and Frameworks

Understanding and selecting the right process model is a critical step in software development. This book delves into various process models, including Waterfall, Evolutionary Development, Component-based Software Engineering, Incremental, and Spiral models. Each model has its strengths and weaknesses, and the choice of model can significantly impact the success of a project. We will also explore process improvement frameworks such as Capability Maturity Model Integration (CMMI), Six Sigma, and Lean Six Sigma, which provide structured approaches to enhancing software processes.

Quality Management Systems

Quality management is a systematic approach to ensuring that software products meet the desired quality standards. This book covers the principles of quality management, including quality assurance, quality control, and the use of standards like ISO 9000. We will also discuss the importance of process measurement and analysis in identifying areas for improvement and tracking progress.

Practical Applications and Case Studies

Theory is essential, but practical application is where the real learning happens. This book includes real-world case studies and examples that illustrate how the concepts discussed can be applied in practice. These case studies highlight the challenges faced by organizations and the strategies they used to overcome them. They provide valuable insights and lessons that can be applied to your own projects.

Future Trends and Challenges

The field of software engineering is constantly evolving, and staying updated with the latest trends and challenges is crucial. This book concludes with a look at future trends in software process improvement and quality management, including emerging technologies and methodologies. We will also discuss the challenges that organizations face in implementing these practices and how they can be addressed.

How to Use This Book

This book is structured to be both modular and progressive. Each chapter builds upon the concepts introduced in the previous ones, allowing readers to follow a logical learning path. However, the modular design also means that readers can easily navigate to specific topics of interest without needing to read the entire book sequentially.

- **For Students**: Use this book as a companion to your coursework. Each chapter includes exercises and questions designed to reinforce key concepts and encourage critical thinking. The real-world examples and case studies will help you see how these principles are applied in practice.

- **For Professionals**: This book serves as a reference guide that you can consult as needed. The detailed explanations and practical advice will help you address challenges in your current projects and stay updated with the latest trends and best practices.

Conclusion

The Software Process Improvement is more than just a textbook; it is a roadmap for navigating the complexities of software development. By providing a solid foundation in the principles and practices of software process improvement and quality management, this book aims to equip you with the knowledge and tools necessary to succeed in the field of software engineering.

Contents

Preface v

Purpose of the Book v

Intended Audience v

How to Use the Book vi

Structure of the Book vi

Additional Resources viii

Acknowledgments viii

Introduction to the Book ix

The Importance of Software Process Improvement.......ix

Strategic Role of Software Quality.....................ix

Continuous Improvement x

Process Models and Frameworks.......................x

Quality Management Systems.............................x

Practical Applications and Case Studies xi

Future Trends and Challenges xi

How to Use This Book..xi

Conclusion xii

Chapter 1: Introduction to Software Process Improvement
....1

1.1 Overview of Software Process Improvement............1

Importance of Software Process Improvement 1

1.2 Strategic Role of Systems and Software Quality 2

Dimensions of Software Quality...............................2

Quality Management Systems 2

1.3 Basic Elements of Continuous Software Process Improvement 3

Process Analysis 3

Process Modeling 3

Process Measurement...4

Process Change Introduction 4

Process Change Training 4

Change Tuning...4

1.4 Key Quotes and Insights.....................................4

1.5 Engineering versus Programming.........................5

The Role of Process in Software Development 5

1.6 Common Software Processes...............................6

Waterfall Model 6

Evolutionary Development...6

Component-based Software Engineering 6

Incremental Model..6

Spiral Model 7

1.7 Conclusion 7

Chapter 2: Software Process Models 8

2.1 Introduction 8

2.2 Waterfall Model 8

2.2.1 Overview 8

2.2.2 Phases of the Waterfall Model.........................8

2.2.3 Advantages..9

2.2.4 Disadvantages 10

2.2.5 Applicability 10

2.3 Evolutionary Development Model 10

2.3.1 Overview 10

2.3.2 Types of Evolutionary Development 10

2.3.3 Advantages...11

2.3.4 Disadvantages 11

2.3.5 Applicability..11

2.4 Component-based Software Engineering (CBSE) 12

2.4.1 Overview 12

2.4.2 Phases of CBSE 12

2.4.3 Advantages...13

2.4.4 Disadvantages 13

2.4.5 Applicability..13

2.5 Incremental Model..13

2.5.1 Overview 13

2.5.2 Phases of the Incremental Model 14

2.5.3 Advantages...15

2.5.4 Disadvantages 15

2.5.5 Applicability..15

2.6 Spiral Model 15

2.6.1 Overview 15

2.6.2 Phases of the Spiral Model............................16

2.6.3 Advantages...16

2.6.4 Disadvantages 17

2.6.5 Applicability..17

2.7 Choosing the Right Model 17

    Key Considerations....................................18

2.8 Conclusion 18

Chapter 3: Software Quality Management 19

    Introduction 19

    The Essence of Software Quality.................19

    Dimensions of Software Quality..............19

    Quality Management Systems (QMS) 20

    Key Components of a QMS 20

    ISO 9000 Standards 21

    Key Features of ISO 9000 21

    Quality Assurance vs. Quality Control............22

    Quality Assurance (QA) 22

    Quality Control (QC)..............................22

    Practical Implementation of Quality Management.......23

    1. Define Quality Goals..........................23

    2. Develop a Quality Plan 23

    3. Implement Quality Assurance Practices.............24

    4. Conduct Quality Control Activities 24

    5. Monitor and Measure Quality Performance.........25

    6. Continuously Improve the Quality Management System...25

    Case Studies and Real-World Examples 26

    Example 1: Company A's Quality Journey 26

    Example 2: Company B's Agile Quality Approach 27

Conclusion 27

Chapter 4: Process Improvement Frameworks................29

Introduction 29

Capability Maturity Model Integration (CMMI) 29

Overview 29

Key Components of CMMI 30

Benefits of CMMI 31

Implementation Challenges 31

Six Sigma 31

Overview 31

Key Components of Six Sigma 32

Benefits of Six Sigma 33

Implementation Challenges 33

Lean Six Sigma 34

Overview 34

Key Components of Lean Six Sigma..........................34

Benefits of Lean Six Sigma................................35

Implementation Challenges 35

Bootstrap Framework 35

Overview 35

Key Components of Bootstrap 36

Benefits of Bootstrap 36

Implementation Challenges 36

Conclusion 37

Chapter 5: Process Analysis and Measurement..............38

Introduction 38

Process Analysis Techniques 38

    Overview 38

    Key Process Analysis Techniques 38

    Benefits of Process Analysis 39

Process Modeling 39

    Overview 39

    Key Process Modeling Techniques 40

    Benefits of Process Modeling..................40

Process Measurement Classes 41

    Overview 41

    Key Process Measurement Classes 41

    Benefits of Process Measurement 42

Goal Question Metric Paradigm.....................42

    Overview 42

    Key Components of GQM...........................42

    Benefits of GQM......................................43

Process Improvement Attributes 43

    Overview 43

    Key Process Improvement Attributes 43

    Benefits of Process Improvement Attributes...........45

Practical Application of Process Analysis and Measurement...45

    1. Define Improvement Objectives 45

    2. Conduct a Baseline Assessment 46

3. Identify Improvement Opportunities 46

4. Develop an Improvement Plan...........................46

5. Implement Changes 46

6. Monitor and Measure Progress..........................46

7. Continuous Improvement 47

Case Studies and Real-World Examples 47

Example 1: Company A's Process Improvement
Journey..47

Example 2: Company B's Agile Transformation.........48

Conclusion 48

Chapter 6: Software Testing Strategies............................50

Introduction 50

Verification and Validation (V&V) 50

Overview 50

Key Concepts of V&V..50

Importance of V&V...51

Levels of Software Testing 51

Overview 51

Key Levels of Software Testing.................................52

Importance of Testing Levels 53

Types of Testing 53

Overview 53

Key Types of Testing...53

Importance of Testing Types....................................54

Testing Techniques and Tools 54

Overview 54

Key Testing Techniques..............................55

Key Testing Tools......................................55

Importance of Testing Techniques and Tools 56

Test Case Design and Management 56

Overview 56

Key Aspects of Test Case Design 57

Key Aspects of Test Case Management 57

Importance of Test Case Design and Management ..58

Practical Application of Software Testing Strategies.....58

1. Define Testing Objectives.......................58

2. Develop a Testing Plan 58

3. Design Test Cases 59

4. Execute Test Cases 59

5. Report and Track Defects 59

6. Continuous Improvement 59

Case Studies and Real-World Examples 59

Example 1: Company A's Testing Transformation.....59

Example 2: Company B's Agile Testing 60

Conclusion 61

Chapter 7: Data Reporting and Analysis............................62

Introduction 62

Data Analytic Strategies 62

Overview 62

Key Data Analytic Strategies........................62

Importance of Data Analytic Strategies 63

Qualitative Data Analysis 64

    Overview 64

    Key Techniques in Qualitative Data Analysis............64

    Importance of Qualitative Data Analysis...................65

Grounded Theory Analysis 65

    Overview 65

    Key Steps in Grounded Theory Analysis...................65

    Importance of Grounded Theory Analysis 66

Interpretation Issues in Qualitative Data Analysis 67

    Overview 67

    Key Interpretation Issues 67

    Importance of Addressing Interpretation Issues.......68

Writing Research Reports 68

    Overview 68

    Key Components of a Research Report...................68

    Importance of Effective Reporting 70

Practical Application of Data Reporting and Analysis ...70

    1. Define Objectives 70

    2. Collect Data 70

    3. Analyze Data....................................70

    4. Interpret Findings...............................71

    5. Write the Report 71

    6. Communicate Results..........................71

    7. Continuous Improvement 71

Case Studies and Real-World Examples 71

Example 1: Company A's Data-Driven Decision-Making..71

Example 2: Company B's Qualitative Insights 72

Conclusion 73

Chapter 8: Systems Development Methodologies............74

Introduction 74

Traditional Systems Development Life Cycle (SDLC).....74

Overview 74

Phases of SDLC 74

Tools and Techniques in SDLC 76

Alternative Methodologies 78

Risk Management in SDLC...78

Overview 78

Key Steps in Risk Management 79

Importance of Risk Management..............................80

Practical Application of Systems Development Methodologies 80

1. Define Project Objectives 80

2. Choose the Right Methodology............................80

3. Plan and Prepare 80

4. Execute the Plan..81

5. Monitor and Control 81

6. Test and Validate...81

7. Implement and Maintain.....................................81

8. Continuous Improvement 81

Case Studies and Real-World Examples 81

Example 1: Company A's SDLC Implementation 81

Example 2: Company B's Agile Transformation.........82

Conclusion 83

Chapter 9: Risk Management and Decision Making 84

Introduction 84

Introduction to Risk Management 84

Overview 84

Key Concepts in Risk Management 84

Importance of Risk Management............................85

Risk Identification and Assessment............................85

Overview 85

Key Steps in Risk Identification and Assessment.......85

Tools and Techniques for Risk Identification and
Assessment 86

Importance of Risk Identification and Assessment ...86

Risk Treatment and Mitigation...................................87

Overview 87

Key Strategies for Risk Treatment and Mitigation 87

Tools and Techniques for Risk Treatment and
Mitigation..88

Importance of Risk Treatment and Mitigation..........88

Enterprise Risk Management (ERM) 88

Overview 88

Key Components of ERM..89

Importance of ERM 90

Strategic Risk Management 90

    Overview 90

    Key Components of Strategic Risk Management 90

    Importance of Strategic Risk Management..............91

Practical Application of Risk Management and Decision Making...91

    1. Define Risk Management Objectives 92

    2. Identify and Assess Risks 92

    3. Develop Risk Treatment Plans..............................92

    4. Implement Risk Mitigation Strategies 92

    5. Monitor and Report on Risks................................92

    6. Continuous Improvement 92

    Case Studies and Real-World Examples 93

    Example 1: Company A's Risk Management Journey93

    Example 2: Company B's Strategic Risk Management 94

    Conclusion..94

Chapter 10: eSourcing Capability Model (eSCM) 96

Introduction 96

The eSourcing Capability Model (eSCM) 96

    Overview 96

    Key Components of eSCM 96

    Benefits of eSCM 98

    Implementation Challenges 99

Practical Application of eSCM 99

    1. Assess Current Capabilities 99

2. Identify Improvement Areas 99

3. Develop an Improvement Plan............................100

4. Implement Changes 100

5. Monitor and Measure Progress 100

6. Continuous Improvement 100

Case Studies and Real-World Examples 100

Example 1: Company A's eSourcing Journey...........100

Example 2: Company B's eSourcing Transformation
....101

Conclusion..102

Chapter 11: ITIL and IT Service Management 103

Introduction 103

The ITIL Framework...103

Overview 103

Key Components of ITIL..103

Benefits of ITIL...106

Implementation Challenges 106

Practical Application of ITIL..107

1. Assess Current IT Practices.................................107

2. Identify Improvement Areas 107

3. Develop an Improvement Plan............................107

4. Implement Changes 107

5. Monitor and Measure Progress 108

6. Continuous Improvement 108

Case Studies and Real-World Examples 108

Example 1: Company A's ITIL Journey 108

Example 2: Company B's ITIL Transformation 109

Conclusion 109

Chapter 12: ISO Standards and Models 111

Introduction 111

The Role of ISO Standards 111

Overview 111

Key ISO Standards for Software Engineering 111

Key ISO Standards for IT Service Management 113

Benefits of ISO Standards..114

Implementation Challenges 114

Practical Application of ISO Standards 115

1. Assess Current Practices....................................115

2. Identify Improvement Areas 115

3. Develop an Improvement Plan...........................115

4. Implement Changes 116

5. Monitor and Measure Progress 116

6. Continuous Improvement 116

Case Studies and Real-World Examples 116

Example 1: Company A's ISO 9001 Journey 116

Example 2: Company B's ISO/IEC 20000
Transformation 117

Conclusion..117

Chapter 13: Case Studies and Practical Applications 119

Introduction 119

Real-world Case Studies 119

Case Study 1: Company A's Agile Transformation...119

Case Study 2: Company B's DevOps Integration 120

Implementation Examples 121

Example 1: Implementing Lean Principles in Software
Development..121

Example 2: Enhancing Security through DevSecOps
....122

Lessons Learned 123

Best Practices and Recommendations 124

Conclusion 125

Chapter 14: Future Trends and Challenges 126

Introduction 126

Emerging Trends in Software Process Improvement..126

Artificial Intelligence and Machine Learning...........126

DevOps and Continuous Integration/Continuous
Deployment (CI/CD) 127

Agile and Lean Methodologies 127

Cloud Computing and Microservices Architecture..127

Internet of Things (IoT) and Embedded Systems 128

Challenges in Implementing Quality Management.....128

Cultural Resistance 128

Resource Constraints 128

Integration with Existing Processes.........................129

Keeping Up with Technological Advancements 129

Measuring and Demonstrating ROI..........................129

Future Directions in Software Engineering 130

Human-Centric Software Engineering....................130

Ethical and Social Implications 130

Sustainability and Green Software Engineering......130

Quantum Computing and Software Development..130

Global Collaboration and Distributed Teams 131

Conclusion 131

Appendix A: Glossary of Terms 133

Agile Methodology..133

Artificial Intelligence (AI)..133

Baseline 133

Capability Maturity Model Integration (CMMI) 133

Cloud Computing...134

Continuous Integration (CI)......................................134

Continuous Deployment (CD) 134

DevOps..134

Enterprise Risk Management (ERM) 135

Grounded Theory 135

Human-Centric Software Engineering........................135

Internet of Things (IoT) 135

Iterative Development 136

Just-In-Time (JIT) Delivery 136

Lean Principles 136

Machine Learning (ML) 136

Microservices Architecture 137

Quality Assurance (QA) 137

Quality Control (QC) 137

Risk Appetite 137

Risk Management 137

Scrum 138

Six Sigma 138

Software Development Life Cycle (SDLC) 138

Stakeholder 138

User-Centric Design....................................139

Value Stream Mapping................................139

Waterfall Model 139

Appendix B: Sample Templates and Forms...................140

Project Plan Template 140

Project Plan Template 140

1. Project Overview 140

2. Project Scope....................................140

3. Deliverables.....................................141

4. Resources 141

5. Schedule 141

6. Risks and Mitigation 141

7. Quality Assurance...............................141

8. Communication Plan 142

9. Approval 142

Test Case Template 142

Test Case Template 142

1. Test Case Information 142

2. Pre-Conditions..143

3. Test Steps 143

4. Expected Results 143

5. Actual Results 143

6. Status...143

7. Notes 143

Risk Assessment Form..144

Risk Assessment Form...144

1. Risk Identification..144

2. Risk Analysis 144

3. Risk Rating 144

4. Risk Mitigation..144

5. Monitoring and Review 145

6. Approval 145

Appendix C: Additional Resources 146

Recommended Reading 146

Useful Websites 147

Tools and Software..149

1. INTRODUCTION TO SOFTWARE PROCESS IMPROVEMENT

1.1 Overview of Software Process Improvement

Software process improvement (SPI) is a strategic approach aimed at enhancing the efficiency, effectiveness, and quality of software development processes. It involves the systematic analysis, evaluation, and enhancement of existing processes to achieve better outcomes in terms of productivity, cost, and quality. SPI is not just about fixing problems; it is about creating a culture of continuous improvement where processes are constantly reviewed and refined to meet evolving needs.

Importance of Software Process Improvement

In the dynamic world of software development, the ability to deliver high-quality software on time and within budget is critical. Software process improvement helps organizations achieve these goals by:

- **Enhancing Predictability**: By standardizing processes, organizations can better predict project outcomes, manage risks, and meet deadlines.
- **Improving Quality**: Systematic process improvements lead to higher quality software that meets user expectations and performs reliably.
- **Increasing Efficiency**: Streamlined processes reduce waste, minimize rework, and optimize resource utilization.

- **Fostering Innovation**: A well-defined process framework allows teams to focus on innovation and continuous improvement.
- **Enhancing Competitiveness**: Organizations that embrace SPI can respond more quickly to market changes and customer needs, giving them a competitive edge.

1.2 Strategic Role of Systems and Software Quality

Software quality is a critical factor in the success of any software project. It encompasses various dimensions, including functionality, reliability, usability, efficiency, maintainability, and portability. High-quality software meets user requirements, performs efficiently, and can be easily maintained and enhanced over time.

Dimensions of Software Quality

- **Functionality**: The software performs the intended functions correctly.
- **Reliability**: The software operates without failure under specified conditions.
- **Usability**: The software is easy to use and understand.
- **Efficiency**: The software performs its tasks with minimal resource consumption.
- **Maintainability**: The software can be easily modified to fix bugs or add new features.
- **Portability**: The software can be easily transferred to different environments or platforms.

Quality Management Systems

Quality management systems (QMS) are frameworks that organizations use to ensure that their products and services meet the desired quality standards. These systems include processes for quality planning, assurance, control, and improvement. Key components of a QMS include:

- **Quality Assurance (QA)**: The process of ensuring that software development processes are followed and that the resulting product meets quality standards.
- **Quality Control (QC)**: The process of verifying that the software product meets specified requirements through testing and inspection.
- **Quality Improvement**: The continuous effort to enhance processes and products based on feedback and performance metrics.

1.3 Basic Elements of Continuous Software Process Improvement

Continuous software process improvement involves a series of steps that ensure processes are constantly reviewed and refined. The basic elements include:

Process Analysis

Process analysis involves a detailed examination of existing processes to identify strengths, weaknesses, and areas for improvement. This can be done through techniques such as process mapping, data collection, and stakeholder interviews.

Process Modeling

Process modeling is the creation of a visual representation of processes to better understand their components and interactions. Models can be used to simulate changes and predict their impact on overall performance.

Process Measurement

Process measurement involves the collection and analysis of data to assess process performance. Metrics such as cycle time, defect rate, and productivity are commonly used to evaluate and improve processes.

Process Change Introduction

Once areas for improvement have been identified, changes are introduced to enhance process efficiency and effectiveness. This may involve adopting new tools, techniques, or methodologies.

Process Change Training

Training is essential to ensure that all team members understand and can effectively implement new processes. This may include workshops, seminars, and hands-on training sessions.

Change Tuning

After implementation, processes need to be continuously monitored and adjusted to ensure they meet the desired objectives. This involves regular reviews and feedback loops to identify and address any issues.

1.4 Key Quotes and Insights

Understanding the importance of software process improvement can be illuminated by the following quotes:

- **"If you don't know where you are going, any road will do."** - Chinese Proverb

- **"If you don't know where you are, a map won't help."** - Watts Humphrey
- **"If you don't know where you are going, a map won't get you there any faster."** - Anonymous
- **"You can't expect to be a functional employee in a dysfunctional environment."** - Watts Humphrey

These quotes emphasize the importance of having a clear direction and a well-defined process to achieve success.

1.5 Engineering versus Programming

While programming focuses on the technical aspects of writing code, engineering involves a broader approach that includes planning, design, testing, and maintenance. Engineers follow established procedures, methods, and standards to ensure more predictable results. This approach is essential for delivering high-quality software that meets user needs and organizational goals.

The Role of Process in Software Development

A well-defined process serves as the foundation for successful software development. It provides a roadmap for the entire development lifecycle, from requirements gathering to deployment and maintenance. By following a structured process, teams can:

- **Ensure Consistency**: Processes ensure that tasks are performed consistently, reducing variability and improving quality.
- **Facilitate Communication**: Clear processes facilitate better communication among team members and stakeholders.
- **Enhance Predictability**: Processes help in predicting project timelines and resource requirements.

- **Support Continuous Improvement**: Processes provide a framework for identifying and implementing improvements.

1.6 Common Software Processes

Understanding the most common software processes is crucial for selecting the right approach for a given project. Some of the widely used processes include:

Waterfall Model

The Waterfall model is a linear, sequential approach where each phase of the software development lifecycle follows the previous one. It is best suited for projects with well-defined requirements and minimal changes.

Evolutionary Development

Evolutionary development involves iterative cycles of development and feedback, allowing for continuous refinement of the software. This approach is ideal for projects with uncertain requirements or those that require rapid prototyping.

Component-based Software Engineering

This approach focuses on the reuse of existing components to build software systems. It reduces development time and enhances reliability by leveraging pre-tested components.

Incremental Model

The Incremental model combines elements of the Waterfall and Evolutionary models. It involves breaking down the software into smaller increments, each of which is developed and tested independently.

Spiral Model

The Spiral model is a hybrid approach that incorporates risk analysis and iterative development. It is particularly useful for large, complex projects where risk management is critical.

1.7 Conclusion

Software process improvement is a strategic initiative that can significantly enhance the efficiency, effectiveness, and quality of software development. By understanding the importance of software quality, adopting a structured process, and continuously seeking improvements, organizations can deliver high-quality software that meets user needs and drives business success. This chapter has provided an overview of the key concepts and elements of software process improvement. The following chapters will delve deeper into specific methodologies, frameworks, and practical applications.

2. SOFTWARE PROCESS MODELS

2.1 Introduction

Software process models are essential tools for understanding and managing the software development lifecycle. They provide a structured approach to developing software, ensuring that all necessary steps are taken to produce high-quality products. This chapter explores various software process models, each with its own strengths and weaknesses, and discusses when and how to apply them effectively.

2.2 Waterfall Model

2.2.1 Overview

The Waterfall model is one of the oldest and most widely recognized software development models. It is a linear, sequential approach where each phase of the software development lifecycle follows the previous one in a strict order. The model is named after the cascading effect of waterfalls, where each phase flows into the next.

2.2.2 Phases of the Waterfall Model

1. **Requirements Gathering and Analysis**

   o Collect and document the requirements of the software.
   o Analyze the requirements to understand the scope and objectives of the project.
2. **System Design**

- Design the architecture of the software system.
- Create detailed design documents and specifications.

3. **Implementation**

  - Write the code based on the design specifications.
  - Develop the software components and integrate them.

4. **Testing**

  - Test the software to identify and fix defects.
  - Conduct unit testing, integration testing, and system testing.

5. **Deployment**

  - Deploy the software to the production environment.
  - Ensure the software is ready for use by end-users.

6. **Maintenance**

  - Provide ongoing support and maintenance.
  - Fix bugs, update features, and enhance the software as needed.

2.2.3 Advantages

- **Structured Approach**: Provides a clear and structured approach to software development.
- **Documentation**: Emphasizes the importance of documentation, which is useful for future reference and maintenance.

- **Predictability**: Helps in predicting project timelines and resource requirements.

2.2.4 Disadvantages

- **Inflexibility**: Difficult to accommodate changes once the project is underway.
- **Late Feedback**: Feedback from users is typically received late in the process, making it hard to incorporate changes.
- **Risk of Failure**: Higher risk of project failure if requirements are not well understood at the beginning.

2.2.5 Applicability

- **Well-Defined Requirements**: Suitable for projects with well-defined and stable requirements.
- **Minimal Changes**: Best for projects where changes are unlikely to occur during development.

2.3 Evolutionary Development Model

2.3.1 Overview

The Evolutionary Development model is an iterative approach that involves continuous refinement of the software based on user feedback. It is particularly useful for projects with uncertain or changing requirements.

2.3.2 Types of Evolutionary Development

1. **Exploratory Development**

   o Focuses on understanding the problem space and exploring potential solutions.

o Often used in the early stages of a project to gather requirements.

2. **Throw-away Prototyping**

   o Involves creating a prototype to understand user needs and gather feedback.
   o The prototype is discarded, and the final product is developed based on the insights gained.

2.3.3 Advantages

- **Flexibility**: Adapts well to changing requirements.
- **Early Feedback**: Provides early feedback from users, allowing for continuous improvement.
- **Reduced Risk**: Reduces the risk of developing a product that does not meet user needs.

2.3.4 Disadvantages

- **Lack of Structure**: Can be less structured and harder to manage.
- **Invisible Process**: May lack clear documentation and structure.
- **Potential for Scope Creep**: Risk of continuous changes leading to scope creep.

2.3.5 Applicability

- **Uncertain Requirements**: Suitable for projects with uncertain or changing requirements.
- **Rapid Prototyping**: Ideal for projects that require quick feedback and iterative development.

2.4 Component-based Software Engineering (CBSE)

2.4.1 Overview

Component-based Software Engineering (CBSE) focuses on the reuse of existing software components to build new systems. This approach leverages pre-built, tested components to reduce development time and enhance reliability.

2.4.2 Phases of CBSE

1. **Requirements Specification**

   - Define the requirements of the software system.
   - Identify the components needed to meet these requirements.

2. **Component Analysis**

   - Analyze existing components to determine their suitability for the project.
   - Select and adapt components as needed.

3. **Development and Integration**

   - Develop any new components required.
   - Integrate the selected components into the system.

4. **System Design with Reuse**

   - Design the system architecture, emphasizing the reuse of components.
   - Ensure that the components work together seamlessly.

5. **System Validation**

- o Validate the integrated system to ensure it meets the specified requirements.
- o Conduct thorough testing to identify and fix defects.

2.4.3 Advantages

- **Reduced Development Time**: Leverages existing components to speed up development.
- **Enhanced Reliability**: Uses pre-tested components, reducing the likelihood of defects.
- **Cost Efficiency**: Reduces the need for extensive development and testing.

2.4.4 Disadvantages

- **Compromises in Requirements**: May require compromises to fit existing components.
- **Less Control**: Less control over the evolution of the system due to reliance on external components.
- **Integration Challenges**: Potential difficulties in integrating components from different sources.

2.4.5 Applicability

- **Component Availability**: Suitable for projects where a pool of existing components is available.
- **Emerging Trends**: Ideal for projects that can benefit from the integration of web services and other reusable components.

2.5 Incremental Model

2.5.1 Overview

The Incremental model combines elements of the Waterfall and Evolutionary models. It involves breaking down the software into smaller increments, each of which is developed and tested independently. This approach allows for early delivery of parts of the system and supports easier integration of subsystems.

2.5.2 Phases of the Incremental Model

1. **Define Outline Requirements**

   - Identify the overall requirements of the software system.
   - Create a high-level specification of the system.

2. **Assign Requirements to Increments**

   - Break down the requirements into smaller, manageable increments.
   - Assign each increment a specific set of requirements.

3. **Develop System Increment**

   - Develop each increment based on the assigned requirements.
   - Conduct unit testing and integration testing for each increment.

4. **Integrate Increment**

   - Integrate the developed increment into the existing system.
   - Conduct system testing to ensure the increment works correctly with the rest of the system.

5. **Validate System**

o Validate the integrated system to ensure it meets the specified requirements.
o Conduct acceptance testing to ensure the system meets user needs.

2.5.3 Advantages

- **Better Support for Iteration**: Provides better support for process iteration and reduces rework.
- **Early Delivery**: Allows for early delivery of parts of the system, enhancing user satisfaction.
- **Lower Risk**: Reduces the risk of project failure by delivering smaller, manageable increments.

2.5.4 Disadvantages

- **Increment Size**: Increments need to be relatively small, which can be challenging to manage.
- **Mapping Requirements**: Mapping requirements to increments may not be straightforward.
- **Common Features**: Identifying common software features can be difficult.

2.5.5 Applicability

- **Part-by-Part Delivery**: Suitable for projects that can be delivered in parts.
- **Complex Systems**: Ideal for complex systems where early feedback and iterative development are beneficial.

2.6 Spiral Model

2.6.1 Overview

The Spiral model is a hybrid approach that incorporates risk analysis and iterative development. It is particularly useful for large, complex projects where risk management is critical. The model is represented as a spiral, with each loop representing a process phase.

2.6.2 Phases of the Spiral Model

1. **Determine Objectives, Alternatives, and Constraints**

   o Define the objectives of the project.
   o Identify alternative solutions and constraints.

2. **Evaluate Alternatives and Identify Risks**

   o Evaluate the alternatives and identify potential risks.
   o Develop risk reduction strategies.

3. **Develop and Verify Next-Level Product**

   o Develop the next level of the product.
   o Verify that the product meets the specified requirements.

4. **Review and Plan Next Phase**

   o Review the progress and results of the current phase.
   o Plan the next phase based on the review and risk assessment.

2.6.3 Advantages

- **Risk Reduction**: Incorporates risk analysis and reduction mechanisms.

- **Iterative Development**: Supports iterative development and reflects real-world practices.
- **Systematic Approach**: Provides a systematic approach to software development.

2.6.4 Disadvantages

- **Complexity**: Can be complex and difficult to follow strictly.
- **Expertise Required**: Requires expertise in risk evaluation and reduction.
- **Applicability**: Best suited for large systems and may not be practical for smaller projects.

2.6.5 Applicability

- **Large Systems**: Ideal for internal development of large systems.
- **Risk Management**: Suitable for projects where risk management is a critical concern.

2.7 Choosing the Right Model

Selecting the appropriate software process model is crucial for the success of a software project. The choice of model depends on various factors, including:

- **Project Requirements**: The nature and complexity of the project requirements.
- **Team Experience**: The experience and expertise of the development team.
- **Resource Availability**: The availability of resources, including time and budget.
- **Risk Management**: The need for risk management and mitigation strategies.

Key Considerations

- **Flexibility**: How well the model can accommodate changes and adapt to evolving requirements.
- **Predictability**: The ability to predict project timelines and resource requirements.
- **Documentation**: The level of documentation and structure provided by the model.
- **User Involvement**: The extent to which the model involves users in the development process.

2.8 Conclusion

Understanding and selecting the right software process model is a critical step in software development. Each model has its own strengths and weaknesses, and the choice of model can significantly impact the success of a project. This chapter has provided an overview of various software process models, including the Waterfall, Evolutionary Development, Component-based Software Engineering, Incremental, and Spiral models. Future chapters will delve deeper into specific methodologies, frameworks, and practical applications to help you make informed decisions in your software development projects.

Certainly! Below is a draft for Chapter 3, balancing narrative explanation with key points to ensure clarity and engagement.

3. SOFTWARE QUALITY MANAGEMENT

Introduction

In the realm of software development, quality is not merely a desirable attribute; it is a fundamental necessity. Software quality management (SQM) is the systematic approach to ensuring that software products meet the desired quality standards. This chapter delves into the principles and practices of software quality management, exploring how it can be effectively integrated into the software development lifecycle to produce reliable, efficient, and user-satisfying software.

The Essence of Software Quality

Software quality is a multifaceted concept that encompasses various dimensions, each contributing to the overall performance and user satisfaction of the software. High-quality software is not just about meeting functional requirements; it also involves reliability, usability, efficiency, maintainability, and portability. These dimensions collectively define the quality of a software product, influencing its acceptance and success in the market.

Dimensions of Software Quality

1. **Functionality**: The software performs the intended functions correctly and meets user requirements.

2. **Reliability**: The software operates without failure under specified conditions, ensuring consistent performance.
3. **Usability**: The software is easy to use and understand, minimizing the learning curve for users.
4. **Efficiency**: The software performs its tasks with minimal resource consumption, optimizing performance.
5. **Maintainability**: The software can be easily modified to fix bugs, add new features, or adapt to changing requirements.
6. **Portability**: The software can be easily transferred to different environments or platforms, ensuring broad applicability.

Quality Management Systems (QMS)

A Quality Management System (QMS) is a structured framework that organizations use to ensure their products and services meet the desired quality standards. QMS encompasses a range of activities, including quality planning, assurance, control, and improvement. These activities are designed to create a culture of quality within the organization, where every aspect of the software development process is scrutinized and refined to achieve excellence.

Key Components of a QMS

1. **Quality Planning**: Establishing quality goals and defining the processes and procedures to achieve them.
2. **Quality Assurance**: Ensuring that the defined quality standards and procedures are followed throughout the development process.

3. **Quality Control**: Monitoring the development process to ensure that the software meets the specified quality requirements.
4. **Quality Improvement**: Continuously identifying areas for improvement and implementing changes to enhance quality.

ISO 9000 Standards

The ISO 9000 family of standards is a widely recognized framework for quality management systems. These standards provide a comprehensive set of guidelines for implementing and maintaining a QMS, ensuring that organizations consistently deliver products and services that meet customer and regulatory requirements.

Key Features of ISO 9000

1. **Customer Focus**: The standards emphasize the importance of understanding and meeting customer needs.
2. **Leadership**: Effective leadership is crucial for driving quality initiatives and ensuring commitment from all levels of the organization.
3. **Engagement of People**: Involving and empowering employees to contribute to quality improvement.
4. **Process Approach**: Managing activities as processes to achieve desired outcomes efficiently and effectively.
5. **Improvement**: Continuously seeking opportunities for improvement to enhance performance.
6. **Evidence-based Decision Making**: Making decisions based on data and information to ensure objectivity and reliability.

7. **Relationship Management**: Building and maintaining strong relationships with suppliers and partners to enhance the overall quality of the product or service.

Quality Assurance vs. Quality Control

Understanding the distinction between quality assurance (QA) and quality control (QC) is essential for effective quality management. While both are integral to ensuring software quality, they serve different purposes and operate at different stages of the development process.

Quality Assurance (QA)

Quality Assurance is a proactive process aimed at ensuring that the software development process adheres to established quality standards and procedures. QA involves activities such as:

- **Developing Quality Plans**: Outlining the quality goals and processes to be followed.
- **Conducting Audits**: Reviewing the development process to ensure compliance with quality standards.
- **Training and Education**: Providing training to team members to enhance their understanding of quality practices.
- **Process Improvement**: Identifying areas for improvement and implementing changes to enhance the overall quality management system.

Quality Control (QC)

Quality Control, on the other hand, is a reactive process focused on verifying that the software product meets the specified quality requirements. QC activities include:

- **Testing**: Conducting various types of testing (e.g., unit testing, integration testing, system testing) to identify defects and ensure functionality.
- **Inspection**: Reviewing software components and documentation to ensure they meet quality standards.
- **Defect Management**: Tracking and managing defects to ensure they are resolved in a timely manner.
- **Corrective Actions**: Implementing corrective actions to address identified issues and prevent recurrence.

Practical Implementation of Quality Management

Implementing a robust quality management system requires a strategic approach that integrates quality practices into every aspect of the software development lifecycle. Here are some practical steps to ensure effective quality management:

1. Define Quality Goals

Clearly define the quality goals for the project, aligning them with customer needs and organizational objectives. These goals should be specific, measurable, achievable, relevant, and time-bound (SMART).

2. Develop a Quality Plan

Create a comprehensive quality plan that outlines the processes, procedures, and tools to be used throughout the development lifecycle. This plan should include:

- **Quality Standards**: Define the quality standards to be followed.
- **Roles and Responsibilities**: Assign roles and responsibilities for quality management activities.
- **Metrics and Measurement**: Establish metrics to measure and monitor quality performance.

3. Implement Quality Assurance Practices

Incorporate quality assurance practices into the development process to ensure adherence to quality standards. This includes:

- **Conducting Regular Audits**: Perform regular audits to assess compliance with quality standards.
- **Providing Training**: Offer training and education to team members to enhance their understanding of quality practices.
- **Encouraging Continuous Improvement**: Foster a culture of continuous improvement by regularly reviewing and refining processes.

4. Conduct Quality Control Activities

Implement quality control activities to verify that the software meets the specified quality requirements. This includes:

- **Testing**: Conduct thorough testing at various stages of the development process to identify and fix defects.

- **Inspection**: Review software components and documentation to ensure they meet quality standards.
- **Defect Management**: Track and manage defects to ensure they are resolved in a timely manner.

5. Monitor and Measure Quality Performance

Regularly monitor and measure quality performance using established metrics. This helps in identifying areas for improvement and ensuring that quality goals are being met. Key metrics may include:

- **Defect Density**: The number of defects per unit of code.
- **Test Coverage**: The percentage of code covered by tests.
- **Customer Satisfaction**: Feedback from users on the quality and usability of the software.

6. Continuously Improve the Quality Management System

Quality management is an ongoing process that requires continuous improvement. Regularly review the quality management system to identify areas for improvement and implement changes to enhance its effectiveness. This includes:

- **Conducting Post-Mortem Reviews**: Perform post-mortem reviews after project completion to identify lessons learned and areas for improvement.
- **Implementing Corrective Actions**: Take corrective actions to address identified issues and prevent recurrence.

- **Updating Quality Standards**: Regularly update quality standards to reflect changes in technology, customer needs, and industry best practices.

Case Studies and Real-World Examples

To illustrate the practical application of software quality management, let's examine a few real-world examples where organizations have successfully implemented quality management systems to enhance their software development processes.

Example 1: Company A's Quality Journey

Company A, a leading software development firm, faced challenges with inconsistent quality and frequent defects in their software products. To address these issues, they implemented a comprehensive quality management system based on the ISO 9000 standards. This involved:

- **Defining Quality Goals**: Setting clear quality goals aligned with customer needs and organizational objectives.
- **Developing a Quality Plan**: Creating a detailed quality plan outlining processes, procedures, and tools.
- **Implementing QA Practices**: Conducting regular audits, providing training, and fostering a culture of continuous improvement.
- **Conducting QC Activities**: Implementing thorough testing, inspection, and defect management processes.
- **Monitoring and Measuring Performance**: Regularly monitoring and measuring quality performance using established metrics.

- **Continuous Improvement**: Continuously reviewing and refining the quality management system to enhance its effectiveness.

As a result of these efforts, Company A saw a significant reduction in defects, improved customer satisfaction, and enhanced overall performance.

Example 2: Company B's Agile Quality Approach

Company B, a startup specializing in mobile application development, adopted an Agile methodology to enhance their development process. They integrated quality management practices into their Agile workflow, ensuring that quality was a continuous focus throughout the development lifecycle. This involved:

- **Iterative Development**: Breaking down the development process into short, iterative cycles to allow for continuous feedback and improvement.
- **Continuous Integration and Testing**: Implementing continuous integration and testing practices to ensure that defects were identified and fixed early in the development process.
- **Collaborative Approach**: Encouraging collaboration among team members and stakeholders to ensure alignment on quality goals and practices.
- **Regular Retrospectives**: Conducting regular retrospectives to identify lessons learned and areas for improvement.

By integrating quality management practices into their Agile workflow, Company B was able to deliver high-quality software products more efficiently and effectively.

Conclusion

Effective software quality management is essential for delivering high-quality software products that meet user expectation.

Certainly! Below is a draft for Chapter 4, balancing narrative explanation with key points to ensure clarity and engagement.

---

4. PROCESS IMPROVEMENT FRAMEWORKS

Introduction

In the dynamic landscape of software development, the quest for continuous improvement is paramount. Process improvement frameworks provide the structured approach necessary to enhance software development processes, ensuring they are more efficient, effective, and capable of delivering high-quality products. This chapter explores several prominent process improvement frameworks, each offering unique methodologies and tools to guide organizations towards achieving their quality and productivity goals.

Capability Maturity Model Integration (CMMI)

Overview

The Capability Maturity Model Integration (CMMI) is a widely recognized framework for improving software development processes. Developed by the Software Engineering Institute (SEI) at Carnegie Mellon University, CMMI provides a comprehensive set of best practices and guidelines to help organizations assess their current processes and identify areas for improvement. By following CMMI, organizations can systematically enhance their software development capabilities, leading to higher quality products and more predictable project outcomes.

Key Components of CMMI

1. **Maturity Levels**: CMMI organizes process improvement into five maturity levels, each representing a different stage of process maturity. These levels range from Initial (Level 1) to Optimizing (Level 5), with each level building upon the previous one.

   - **Level 1: Initial**: Processes are typically ad hoc and chaotic.
   - **Level 2: Managed**: Processes are planned and controlled, and projects meet their requirements.
   - **Level 3: Defined**: Processes are well-defined and documented, and the organization has a standard set of processes.
   - **Level 4: Quantitatively Managed**: Processes are measured and controlled based on quantitative data.
   - **Level 5: Optimizing**: The organization focuses on continuous process improvement through innovation and defect prevention.

2. **Process Areas**: CMMI identifies specific process areas that organizations should address to achieve each maturity level. These areas cover various aspects of software development, such as requirements management, project planning, and quality assurance.

3. **Specific and Generic Goals**: Each process area has specific goals that organizations must achieve to demonstrate maturity. Additionally, generic goals apply to all process areas, ensuring that processes are institutionalized and consistently followed.

Benefits of CMMI

- **Predictability**: CMMI helps organizations achieve more predictable project outcomes by standardizing processes.
- **Quality Improvement**: By following best practices, organizations can deliver higher quality software products.
- **Risk Reduction**: CMMI's structured approach helps identify and mitigate risks early in the development process.
- **Competitive Advantage**: Organizations that achieve higher CMMI maturity levels often gain a competitive edge in the market.

Implementation Challenges

- **Resource Intensive**: Implementing CMMI can be resource-intensive, requiring significant time and effort.
- **Cultural Resistance**: Organizations may face resistance from employees who are accustomed to existing processes.
- **Complexity**: The framework's complexity can make it challenging to implement and maintain.

Six Sigma

Overview

Six Sigma is a data-driven methodology aimed at improving the quality of processes by identifying and eliminating defects. Developed by Motorola in the 1980s, Six Sigma has since been adopted by numerous organizations across various industries. The methodology focuses on reducing variation and achieving near-perfect performance, with the ultimate goal of achieving a defect rate of 3.4 defects per million opportunities (DPMO).

Key Components of Six Sigma

1. **DMAIC**: The DMAIC (Define, Measure, Analyze, Improve, Control) framework is a structured problem-solving approach used to improve existing processes.

   o **Define**: Identify the problem and set clear objectives.
   o **Measure**: Collect data to understand the current performance.
   o **Analyze**: Analyze the data to identify root causes of defects.
   o **Improve**: Develop and implement solutions to address the root causes.
   o **Control**: Monitor the process to ensure improvements are sustained.

2. **DMADV**: The DMADV (Define, Measure, Analyze, Design, Verify) framework is used for designing new products or processes to meet customer requirements.

   o **Define**: Define the project goals and customer requirements.
   o **Measure**: Measure the current process and identify gaps.
   o **Analyze**: Analyze the data to identify opportunities for improvement.
   o **Design**: Design a new process or product to meet the requirements.

o **Verify**: Verify the effectiveness of the new design.

3. **Six Sigma Belts**: Six Sigma practitioners are certified at different levels, known as belts, based on their expertise and role in the organization.

   o **Green Belt**: Entry-level practitioners who focus on specific projects.
   o **Black Belt**: Experienced practitioners who lead Six Sigma projects.
   o **Master Black Belt**: Experts who mentor and train other practitioners.

Benefits of Six Sigma

- **Quality Improvement**: Six Sigma helps organizations achieve significant improvements in quality by reducing defects.
- **Cost Reduction**: By eliminating waste and improving efficiency, Six Sigma can lead to substantial cost savings.
- **Customer Satisfaction**: Improved quality and reduced defects lead to higher customer satisfaction.
- **Data-Driven Decision Making**: Six Sigma emphasizes the use of data and statistical analysis to make informed decisions.

Implementation Challenges

- **Cultural Resistance**: Implementing Six Sigma may face resistance from employees who are not accustomed to data-driven decision making.
- **Expertise Requirement**: Successful implementation requires trained and certified practitioners.

- **Time and Resource Intensive**: Implementing Six Sigma can be time-consuming and resource-intensive.

Lean Six Sigma

Overview

Lean Six Sigma combines the principles of Lean methodology, which focuses on eliminating waste, with the defect reduction techniques of Six Sigma. This integrated approach aims to improve process efficiency and quality by addressing both process waste and variation. Lean Six Sigma is particularly effective in environments where both efficiency and quality are critical.

Key Components of Lean Six Sigma

1. **Lean Principles**: Focus on identifying and eliminating waste in processes.

   o **Value Stream Mapping**: Visualize and analyze the flow of materials and information.
   o **5S**: Sort, Set in Order, Shine, Standardize, and Sustain to create a clean and efficient workspace.
   o **Just-In-Time (JIT)**: Produce and deliver products just in time to reduce inventory and waste.

2. **Six Sigma Techniques**: Apply DMAIC and DMADV frameworks to reduce defects and variation.

   o **Statistical Tools**: Use tools like control charts, Pareto charts, and hypothesis testing to analyze data.

    o **Root Cause Analysis**: Identify and address the root causes of problems to prevent recurrence.

Benefits of Lean Six Sigma

- **Efficiency Improvement**: Lean Six Sigma helps organizations streamline processes and eliminate waste.
- **Quality Enhancement**: By reducing defects and variation, Lean Six Sigma improves product quality.
- **Customer Focus**: The methodology emphasizes meeting customer needs and expectations.
- **Holistic Approach**: Combining Lean and Six Sigma provides a comprehensive approach to process improvement.

Implementation Challenges

- **Complexity**: Implementing Lean Six Sigma can be complex, requiring a deep understanding of both Lean and Six Sigma principles.
- **Resistance to Change**: Organizations may face resistance from employees who are accustomed to existing processes.
- **Resource Allocation**: Successful implementation requires dedicated resources and time.

Bootstrap Framework

Overview

The Bootstrap framework is designed for small and medium-sized organizations that may not have the resources to implement larger, more complex process improvement frameworks like CMMI. Bootstrap provides a practical and flexible approach to process improvement, focusing on incremental changes and continuous improvement.

Key Components of Bootstrap

1. **Incremental Improvement**: Bootstrap emphasizes making small, incremental changes to processes, allowing organizations to gradually improve over time.
2. **Practical Tools**: The framework provides practical tools and techniques that are easy to implement and understand.
3. **Flexibility**: Bootstrap is designed to be flexible, allowing organizations to tailor the framework to their specific needs and circumstances.

Benefits of Bootstrap

- **Accessibility**: Bootstrap is accessible to small and medium-sized organizations with limited resources.
- **Practicality**: The framework provides practical tools and techniques that are easy to implement.
- **Incremental Change**: Organizations can make small, incremental changes to processes, making the transition smoother.

Implementation Challenges

- **Limited Scope**: Bootstrap may not be suitable for larger organizations with more complex needs.
- **Resource Constraints**: Small organizations may still face resource constraints in implementing the framework.

- **Sustainability**: Ensuring the sustainability of improvements can be challenging without dedicated resources.

Conclusion

Process improvement frameworks like CMMI, Six Sigma, Lean Six Sigma, and Bootstrap provide structured approaches to enhancing software development processes. Each framework offers unique methodologies and tools to guide organizations towards achieving their quality and productivity goals. By understanding the strengths and challenges of these frameworks, organizations can select the approach that best aligns with their needs and capabilities. Implementing a process improvement framework requires commitment, resources, and a willingness to change, but the benefits in terms of quality, efficiency, and customer satisfaction can be substantial.

5. PROCESS ANALYSIS AND MEASUREMENT

Introduction

In the realm of software development, understanding and improving processes is crucial for delivering high-quality products efficiently. Process analysis and measurement provide the tools and techniques necessary to evaluate existing processes, identify areas for improvement, and implement changes that enhance overall performance. This chapter delves into the methodologies and practices of process analysis and measurement, exploring how they can be applied to achieve continuous improvement in software development.

Process Analysis Techniques

Overview

Process analysis is the systematic examination of existing processes to understand their strengths, weaknesses, and areas for improvement. Effective process analysis involves a combination of qualitative and quantitative techniques to gain a comprehensive understanding of process performance.

Key Process Analysis Techniques

1. **Process Mapping**: Creating visual representations of processes to identify inefficiencies and bottlenecks.

- o **Activity Diagrams**: Visual representations of process activities and their interactions.
- o **Flowcharts**: Diagrams that illustrate the sequence of steps in a process.
- o **Value Stream Mapping**: A tool used to identify and eliminate waste in processes.
2. **Stakeholder Interviews**: Engaging with stakeholders to gather insights and feedback on existing processes.

- o **Structured Interviews**: Formal interviews with predefined questions.
- o **Focus Groups**: Group discussions to gather diverse perspectives.
3. **Data Collection**: Gathering data on process performance to support informed decision-making.

- o **Automated Tools**: Software tools that collect data on process metrics.
- o **Manual Logging**: Recording data through manual processes.

Benefits of Process Analysis

- **Identifies Inefficiencies**: Helps in identifying areas where processes can be streamlined.
- **Enhances Understanding**: Provides a clear understanding of process workflows and interactions.
- **Supports Decision-Making**: Offers data-driven insights to support process improvement initiatives.

Process Modeling

Overview

Process modeling involves creating structured representations of processes to facilitate understanding and improvement. Models can be used to simulate changes and predict their impact on overall performance.

Key Process Modeling Techniques

1. **Activity Diagrams**: Visual representations of process activities and their interactions.

   o **UML (Unified Modeling Language)**: A standardized notation for modeling software systems.
   o **BPMN (Business Process Model and Notation)**: A notation for specifying business processes in a workflow.

2. **Flowcharts**: Diagrams that illustrate the sequence of steps in a process.

   o **High-Level Flowcharts**: Provide an overview of the process.
   o **Detailed Flowcharts**: Offer a granular view of process activities.

3. **Simulation Models**: Models that simulate process performance under various conditions.

   o **Discrete Event Simulation**: Simulates the behavior of processes over time.
   o **System Dynamics**: Models that simulate the behavior of complex systems.

Benefits of Process Modeling

- **Facilitates Understanding**: Helps stakeholders understand complex processes.

- **Supports Change Management**: Provides a basis for simulating and evaluating process changes.
- **Enhances Communication**: Serves as a common language for discussing process improvements.

Process Measurement Classes

Overview

Process measurement involves collecting and analyzing data to assess process performance. Metrics are used to quantify process attributes and identify areas for improvement.

Key Process Measurement Classes

1. **Time-Based Metrics**: Metrics that measure the time taken to complete process activities.

    - **Cycle Time**: The time taken to complete a process.
    - **Lead Time**: The time from the start of a process to its completion.

2. **Resource-Based Metrics**: Metrics that measure the resources required to complete processes.

    - **Person-Months**: The amount of effort required to complete a process.
    - **Cost**: The financial resources required to complete a process.

3. **Event-Based Metrics**: Metrics that measure the occurrence of specific events.

    - **Defect Density**: The number of defects per unit of code.

o   **Incident Rate**: The number of incidents reported per unit of time.

Benefits of Process Measurement

- **Quantifies Performance**: Provides a quantitative basis for evaluating process performance.
- **Identifies Areas for Improvement**: Highlights areas where processes can be improved.
- **Supports Decision-Making**: Offers data-driven insights to support process improvement initiatives.

Goal Question Metric Paradigm

Overview

The Goal Question Metric (GQM) Paradigm is a structured approach to defining and using metrics to achieve specific goals. It involves defining goals, formulating questions to address those goals, and selecting metrics to answer those questions.

Key Components of GQM

1. **Goals**: Clearly defined objectives that the metrics aim to achieve.

   o   **Example**: Improve software reliability by reducing the number of defects.

2. **Questions**: Specific questions formulated to address the goals.

   o   **Example**: What is the current defect density in our software?

3. **Metrics**: Quantifiable measures selected to answer the questions.

- o **Example**: Defect density per thousand lines of code.

Benefits of GQM

- **Aligns Metrics with Goals**: Ensures that metrics are directly related to organizational goals.
- **Facilitates Communication**: Provides a clear framework for discussing and understanding metrics.
- **Supports Continuous Improvement**: Helps in identifying and addressing areas for improvement.

Process Improvement Attributes

Overview

Process improvement attributes are characteristics that describe the quality and effectiveness of a process. These attributes help in evaluating and enhancing process performance.

Key Process Improvement Attributes

1. **Understandability**: The degree to which a process is well defined and understood.

   - o **Clear Documentation**: Processes are clearly documented and easy to understand.
   - o **Training and Education**: Team members are trained to understand and follow the process.
2. **Visibility**: Process activities have results that are externally recognizable.

- o **Transparent Processes**: Processes are transparent, and their results are visible to stakeholders.
- o **Reporting and Dashboards**: Regular reporting and dashboards to communicate process performance.
3. **Supportability**: Process activities supported by tools and technologies.

- o **Automated Tools**: Use of automated tools to support process activities.
- o **Integration with Other Systems**: Processes are integrated with other systems and tools.
4. **Acceptability**: Defined processes are used and accepted by software engineers.

- o **Adoption and Compliance**: Team members adopt and comply with defined processes.
- o **Feedback Mechanisms**: Mechanisms for gathering feedback on process effectiveness.
5. **Reliability**: Process is defined so that errors are avoided or trapped before product errors result.

- o **Error Detection and Correction**: Processes include mechanisms for detecting and correcting errors.
- o **Quality Control**: Regular quality control checks to ensure process reliability.
6. **Robustness**: Process can continue despite unexpected problems.

- o **Contingency Planning**: Processes include contingency plans for unexpected problems.
- o **Resilience**: Processes are resilient to disruptions and can recover quickly.

7. **Maintainability**: Process can evolve to reflect changing organizational requirements or identified process improvements.

   o **Continuous Improvement**: Processes are regularly reviewed and improved.
   o **Adaptability**: Processes can be adapted to changing requirements.

8. **Rapidity**: The time required to complete a system from specification to delivery.

   o **Efficient Processes**: Processes are efficient and minimize delays.
   o **Time-to-Market**: Processes support rapid delivery of products and services.

Benefits of Process Improvement Attributes

- **Enhances Process Quality**: Helps in identifying and enhancing the quality of processes.
- **Supports Continuous Improvement**: Provides a framework for ongoing process enhancement.
- **Improves Stakeholder Satisfaction**: Ensures that processes meet stakeholder expectations and needs.

Practical Application of Process Analysis and Measurement

To effectively implement process analysis and measurement, organizations should follow a structured approach. Here are the steps to achieve successful process improvement:

1. Define Improvement Objectives

Start by defining clear, specific objectives for process improvement. These objectives should align with organizational goals and be measurable and achievable.

2. Conduct a Baseline Assessment

Perform a baseline assessment of current processes to establish a starting point for improvement. This involves collecting data, mapping processes, and identifying inefficiencies.

3. Identify Improvement Opportunities

Based on the baseline assessment, identify specific areas for improvement. This may involve enhancing certain practices, implementing new processes, or improving existing ones.

4. Develop an Improvement Plan

Create a detailed improvement plan that outlines the steps needed to achieve the desired objectives. This plan should include specific actions, timelines, and responsible parties.

5. Implement Changes

Implement the identified changes, ensuring that they are aligned with organizational goals. This may involve training employees, updating processes, and introducing new tools or technologies.

6. Monitor and Measure Progress

Regularly monitor and measure progress using established metrics and performance indicators. This helps ensure that improvements are sustained and that the organization continues to move towards higher performance.

7. Continuous Improvement

Adopt a culture of continuous improvement, where processes are regularly reviewed and refined based on performance data and feedback. This ensures that the organization remains agile and responsive to changing needs and market conditions.

Case Studies and Real-World Examples

Example 1: Company A's Process Improvement Journey

Company A, a software development firm, faced challenges with inconsistent quality and frequent delays in project delivery. To address these issues, the company initiated a process improvement program, starting with a thorough assessment of its current development processes. They identified several areas for improvement, including inefficient requirements gathering, inadequate testing practices, and poor project management.

Based on the assessment, Company A developed a comprehensive improvement plan that included enhancing requirements management practices, implementing automated testing tools, and adopting Agile methodologies for project management. They conducted pilot tests to assess the impact of these changes and then rolled them out across the organization.

By following a structured approach to process improvement, Company A achieved significant improvements in its development processes. They saw a reduction in project cycle times, improved software quality, and increased customer satisfaction. The process improvement program also fostered a culture of continuous improvement, enabling the organization to adapt to changing needs and market conditions.

Example 2: Company B's Agile Transformation

Company B, a global IT service provider, sought to improve its software development processes to better meet customer needs and enhance productivity. The company decided to adopt Agile methodologies, which emphasize iterative development, customer collaboration, and continuous improvement.

To implement Agile, Company B conducted training sessions for its development teams, introduced Agile tools and practices, and restructured its project management processes. They also established metrics to measure the impact of Agile adoption, such as cycle time, defect density, and customer satisfaction.

By embracing Agile methodologies, Company B achieved significant improvements in its software development processes. They saw faster project delivery times, improved software quality, and increased customer satisfaction. The Agile transformation also enhanced the organization's ability to respond to changing requirements and market conditions, fostering a culture of continuous improvement.

Conclusion

Process analysis and measurement are essential tools for understanding, controlling, and improving software development processes. By defining clear improvement objectives, conducting a baseline assessment, identifying opportunities for improvement, developing an improvement plan, implementing changes, monitoring progress, and fostering continuous improvement, organizations can systematically enhance their development processes.

Implementing process analysis and measurement requires commitment, resources, and a willingness to change, but the benefits in terms of enhanced performance, reduced risks, and increased stakeholder satisfaction are substantial. Through practical application and ongoing refinement, organizations can leverage process analysis and measurement to achieve significant advancements in their software development capabilities and overall performance.

CHAPTER 6: SOFTWARE TESTING STRATEGIES

Introduction

In the realm of software development, ensuring that the final product meets the specified requirements and performs reliably is paramount. Software testing strategies play a crucial role in achieving this goal. This chapter explores the principles and practices of software testing, focusing on verification and validation (V&V), levels of software testing, types of testing, testing techniques and tools, and test case design and management. By understanding and applying these strategies, organizations can deliver high-quality software products that meet user expectations.

Verification and Validation (V&V)

Overview

Verification and Validation (V&V) are critical processes in software development that ensure the software product meets the specified requirements and performs as intended. Verification is the process of evaluating the work product to determine if it meets its specified requirements, while validation ensures that the product fulfills the user's expectations.

Key Concepts of V&V

1. **Verification:**

- o **Definition**: Evaluation of an object to demonstrate that it meets its specification.
- o **Purpose**: Ensures that the product is built correctly.
- o **Activities**: Reviews, walkthroughs, inspections, and static analysis.

2. **Validation:**

- o **Definition**: Evaluation of an object to demonstrate that it meets the customer's expectations.
- o **Purpose**: Ensures that the correct product is built.
- o **Activities**: Dynamic testing, user acceptance testing, and performance testing.

Importance of V&V

- **Quality Assurance**: V&V processes help ensure that the software is of high quality and meets user requirements.
- **Risk Reduction**: By identifying defects early, V&V reduces the risk of delivering a faulty product.
- **Customer Satisfaction**: Ensures that the final product meets user expectations, leading to higher satisfaction.

Levels of Software Testing

Overview

Software testing is conducted at various levels to ensure that different aspects of the software are thoroughly examined. Each level of testing focuses on specific aspects of the software, from individual components to the entire system.

Key Levels of Software Testing

1. **Unit Testing**:

   o **Definition**: Testing individual components or units of the software.
   o **Purpose**: Ensures that each unit of the software works correctly.
   o **Activities**: Writing and running test cases for individual functions, methods, or classes.

2. **Integration Testing**:

   o **Definition**: Testing the combined units to ensure they work together.
   o **Purpose**: Ensures that the integrated system functions correctly.
   o **Activities**: Testing interfaces between units, data flow, and interaction.

3. **System Testing**:

   o **Definition**: Testing the complete, integrated system to ensure it meets specified requirements.
   o **Purpose**: Ensures that the entire system works as intended.
   o **Activities**: Testing the system as a whole, including performance, usability, and security.

4. **Acceptance Testing**:

   o **Definition**: Testing to determine if the software meets the acceptance criteria.

- o **Purpose**: Ensures that the software is ready for delivery and meets user requirements.
- o **Activities**: User acceptance testing, alpha testing, and beta testing.

Importance of Testing Levels

- **Early Defect Detection**: Identifies defects early in the development process, reducing the cost of fixing them.
- **Comprehensive Coverage**: Ensures that all aspects of the software are tested.
- **User Confidence**: Provides assurance that the software meets user expectations and requirements.

Types of Testing

Overview

Different types of testing focus on specific aspects of the software, ensuring comprehensive coverage and reliability. Each type of testing serves a unique purpose and is essential for delivering high-quality software.

Key Types of Testing

1. **Functional Testing**:

   - o **Definition**: Testing the functionality of the software.
   - o **Purpose**: Ensures that the software performs its intended functions.
   - o **Activities**: Testing specific features, user stories, and use cases.

2. **Non-Functional Testing**:

- o **Definition**: Testing the performance, reliability, and usability of the software.
- o **Purpose**: Ensures that the software meets non-functional requirements.
- o **Activities**: Performance testing, load testing, stress testing, and usability testing.

3. **Regression Testing**:

- o **Definition**: Testing to ensure that changes or fixes do not affect existing functionality.
- o **Purpose**: Ensures that new changes do not introduce new defects.
- o **Activities**: Re-running test cases to verify that existing functionality remains intact.

4. **Security Testing**:

- o **Definition**: Testing to ensure the software is secure and protected from threats.
- o **Purpose**: Ensures that the software is free from vulnerabilities.
- o **Activities**: Penetration testing, vulnerability scanning, and security audits.

Importance of Testing Types

- **Comprehensive Coverage**: Ensures that all aspects of the software are tested.
- **User Confidence**: Provides assurance that the software is reliable and secure.
- **Risk Reduction**: Identifies and mitigates potential risks associated with software defects.

Testing Techniques and Tools

Overview

Effective testing requires the use of appropriate techniques and tools to ensure thorough and efficient testing. Testing techniques provide structured approaches to designing and executing test cases, while tools automate and streamline the testing process.

Key Testing Techniques

1. **Black-Box Testing**:

   - **Definition**: Testing the software without knowledge of its internal structure.
   - **Purpose**: Ensures that the software meets functional requirements.
   - **Activities**: Equivalence partitioning, boundary value analysis, and decision table testing.

2. **White-Box Testing**:

   - **Definition**: Testing the internal structure and workings of the software.
   - **Purpose**: Ensures that the software is free from defects in its internal logic.
   - **Activities**: Statement coverage, branch coverage, and path coverage.

3. **Gray-Box Testing**:

   - **Definition**: Testing with partial knowledge of the internal structure.
   - **Purpose**: Combines the benefits of black-box and white-box testing.
   - **Activities**: Testing interfaces and internal data structures.

Key Testing Tools

1. **Automated Testing Tools**:

   o **Definition**: Tools that automate the execution of test cases.
   o **Purpose**: Increases efficiency and reduces the risk of human error.
   o **Examples**: Selenium, JUnit, TestNG.

2. **Performance Testing Tools**:

   o **Definition**: Tools that measure the performance of the software.
   o **Purpose**: Ensures that the software meets performance requirements.
   o **Examples**: JMeter, LoadRunner, Gatling.

3. **Static Analysis Tools**:

   o **Definition**: Tools that analyze the source code without executing it.
   o **Purpose**: Identifies potential defects and vulnerabilities in the code.
   o **Examples**: SonarQube, Checkmarx, ESLint.

Importance of Testing Techniques and Tools

- **Efficiency**: Automates repetitive tasks, increasing the speed of testing.
- **Accuracy**: Reduces the risk of human error in test execution.
- **Comprehensive Coverage**: Ensures that all aspects of the software are tested.

Test Case Design and Management

Overview

Test case design and management are critical components of the testing process. Effective test case design ensures that test cases are comprehensive and cover all aspects of the software. Test case management involves organizing, tracking, and maintaining test cases throughout the testing lifecycle.

Key Aspects of Test Case Design

1. **Test Case Design Techniques:**

   - **Equivalence Partitioning**: Dividing input data into partitions to reduce the number of test cases.
   - **Boundary Value Analysis**: Testing boundary values to identify defects.
   - **Decision Table Testing**: Using decision tables to design test cases.

2. **Test Case Writing:**

   - **Preconditions**: Conditions that must be met before the test case can be executed.
   - **Test Steps**: Detailed steps to execute the test case.
   - **Expected Results**: Expected outcomes of the test case.

Key Aspects of Test Case Management

1. **Test Case Organization:**

   - **Categorization**: Organizing test cases into categories based on functionality or requirements.
   - **Prioritization**: Prioritizing test cases based on their importance and impact.

2. **Test Case Tracking**:

   o **Execution Status**: Tracking the execution status of test cases.
   o **Defect Tracking**: Tracking defects identified during test execution.

3. **Test Case Maintenance**:

   o **Updating Test Cases**: Updating test cases to reflect changes in the software.
   o **Retiring Test Cases**: Retiring test cases that are no longer relevant.

Importance of Test Case Design and Management

- **Comprehensive Coverage**: Ensures that all aspects of the software are tested.
- **Efficiency**: Reduces the number of test cases needed to achieve comprehensive coverage.
- **Traceability**: Ensures that test cases are traceable to requirements and defects.

Practical Application of Software Testing Strategies

To effectively implement software testing strategies, organizations should follow a structured approach. Here are the steps to achieve successful testing:

1. Define Testing Objectives

Start by defining clear, specific objectives for testing. These objectives should align with organizational goals and be measurable and achievable.

2. Develop a Testing Plan

Create a detailed testing plan that outlines the scope, resources, and schedule for testing. This plan should include the types of testing to be performed, the tools to be used, and the roles and responsibilities of team members.

3. Design Test Cases

Design comprehensive test cases using appropriate techniques such as equivalence partitioning, boundary value analysis, and decision table testing. Ensure that test cases cover all aspects of the software.

4. Execute Test Cases

Execute test cases using automated tools where possible to increase efficiency and reduce the risk of human error. Track the execution status and record any defects identified.

5. Report and Track Defects

Report identified defects and track their resolution. Use defect tracking tools to manage the defect lifecycle.

6. Continuous Improvement

Adopt a culture of continuous improvement, where testing processes are regularly reviewed and refined based on performance data and feedback. This ensures that the organization remains agile and responsive to changing needs and market conditions.

Case Studies and Real-World Examples

Example 1: Company A's Testing Transformation

Company A, a software development firm, faced challenges with inconsistent quality and frequent defects in their software products. To address these issues, the company initiated a comprehensive testing program, starting with defining clear testing objectives and developing a detailed testing plan. They designed comprehensive test cases using equivalence partitioning and boundary value analysis and executed these test cases using automated tools.

By following a structured approach to testing, Company A achieved significant improvements in their software quality. They saw a reduction in the number of defects, improved user satisfaction, and faster time-to-market for their products.

Example 2: Company B's Agile Testing

Company B, a global IT service provider, sought to improve its software development processes to better meet customer needs and enhance productivity. The company decided to adopt Agile methodologies, which emphasize iterative development, customer collaboration, and continuous improvement.

To implement Agile testing, Company B conducted training sessions for its development teams, introduced automated testing tools, and restructured its testing processes to align with Agile principles. They designed test cases using decision table testing and executed these test cases using automated tools.

By embracing Agile testing, Company B achieved significant improvements in its software development processes. They saw faster project delivery times, improved software quality, and increased customer satisfaction. The Agile testing transformation also enhanced the organization's ability to respond to changing requirements and market conditions.

Conclusion

Software testing strategies are essential for ensuring that software products meet specified requirements and perform reliably. By understanding and applying verification and validation processes, conducting testing at various levels, using appropriate testing techniques and tools, and managing test cases effectively, organizations can deliver high-quality software products. Implementing these strategies requires commitment, resources, and a willingness to change, but the benefits in terms of enhanced performance, reduced risks, and increased stakeholder satisfaction are substantial. Through practical application and ongoing refinement, organizations can leverage software testing strategies to achieve significant advancements in their software development capabilities and overall performance.

CHAPTER 7: DATA REPORTING AND ANALYSIS

Introduction

In the realm of software development and IT service management, data is a valuable asset that can provide deep insights into process performance, user satisfaction, and areas for improvement. Effective data reporting and analysis are crucial for transforming raw data into actionable information that can drive decision-making and enhance organizational performance. This chapter explores the principles and practices of data reporting and analysis, focusing on data analytic strategies, qualitative data analysis, grounded theory analysis, interpretation issues, and writing research reports.

Data Analytic Strategies

Overview

Data analytic strategies are systematic approaches to examining and interpreting data to extract meaningful insights. These strategies help organizations make informed decisions, identify trends, and evaluate the effectiveness of their processes and products.

Key Data Analytic Strategies

1. **Descriptive Analytics:**

    o **Definition**: Summarizing and describing the features of a dataset.

- **Purpose**: Provides a clear picture of what has happened.
- **Activities**: Calculating measures such as mean, median, mode, and standard deviation.

2. **Diagnostic Analytics**:

- **Definition**: Identifying the root causes of issues or trends.
- **Purpose**: Helps in understanding why something happened.
- **Activities**: Root cause analysis, correlation analysis, and drill-down analysis.

3. **Predictive Analytics**:

- **Definition**: Using historical data to predict future outcomes.
- **Purpose**: Forecasts future trends and behaviors.
- **Activities**: Regression analysis, time series analysis, and machine learning models.

4. **Prescriptive Analytics**:

- **Definition**: Providing recommendations for actions based on predictive analytics.
- **Purpose**: Guides decision-making by suggesting the best course of action.
- **Activities**: Optimization algorithms, simulation models, and decision trees.

Importance of Data Analytic Strategies

- **Informed Decision-Making**: Provides data-driven insights to support strategic decisions.

- **Performance Improvement**: Identifies areas for improvement and tracks progress.
- **Risk Management**: Helps in identifying potential risks and implementing proactive measures.

Qualitative Data Analysis

Overview

Qualitative data analysis involves examining and interpreting non-numerical data, such as text, images, and videos, to understand underlying themes and patterns. This type of analysis is particularly useful for gaining deep insights into user experiences, perceptions, and behaviors.

Key Techniques in Qualitative Data Analysis

1. **Coding**:

   o **Definition**: Assigning labels or codes to data to identify themes and patterns.
   o **Purpose**: Organizes data into manageable units for further analysis.
   o **Activities**: Open coding, axial coding, and selective coding.

2. **Content Analysis**:

   o **Definition**: Systematic examination of the content of text data.
   o **Purpose**: Identifies patterns, themes, and trends in the data.
   o **Activities**: Frequency analysis, thematic analysis, and sentiment analysis.

3. **Narrative Analysis**:

- o **Definition**: Examining and interpreting stories and narratives.
- o **Purpose**: Understands the meaning and context of user experiences.
- o **Activities**: Identifying plot structures, character roles, and narrative themes.

Importance of Qualitative Data Analysis

- **Deep Insights**: Provides rich, detailed insights into user experiences and perceptions.
- **Contextual Understanding**: Helps in understanding the context and meaning behind data.
- **User-Centric Design**: Supports the development of user-centric products and services.

Grounded Theory Analysis

Overview

Grounded theory analysis is a qualitative research method that aims to develop theories grounded in the data. It involves systematically collecting and analyzing data to identify patterns and generate theories.

Key Steps in Grounded Theory Analysis

1. **Data Collection**:

   - o **Definition**: Gathering data through interviews, observations, and other methods.
   - o **Purpose**: Provides the raw material for analysis.
   - o **Activities**: Conducting interviews, focus groups, and observations.

2. **Open Coding**:

- o **Definition**: Breaking down data into discrete parts and labeling them.
- o **Purpose**: Identifies initial codes and categories.
- o **Activities**: Line-by-line coding, memoing, and constant comparison.

3. **Axial Coding:**

- o **Definition**: Relating codes to each other to form categories.
- o **Purpose**: Develops a more structured understanding of the data.
- o **Activities**: Making connections between codes, identifying properties and dimensions.

4. **Selective Coding:**

- o **Definition**: Integrating categories into a coherent theory.
- o **Purpose**: Generates a grounded theory.
- o **Activities**: Identifying the core category, integrating categories, and writing the theory.

Importance of Grounded Theory Analysis

- **Theory Development**: Generates theories that are grounded in empirical data.
- **Rich Insights**: Provides deep, context-specific insights into complex phenomena.
- **Flexibility**: Adapts to the data, allowing for the emergence of unexpected findings.

Interpretation Issues in Qualitative Data Analysis

Overview

Interpreting qualitative data can be challenging due to its subjective nature. Researchers must be aware of potential biases and ensure that their interpretations are grounded in the data.

Key Interpretation Issues

1. **Researcher Bias:**

    o **Definition**: The influence of the researcher's preconceptions and biases on data interpretation.
    o **Purpose**: Ensures that interpretations are objective and grounded in the data.
    o **Activities**: Reflexivity, triangulation, and peer debriefing.

2. **Data Saturation:**

    o **Definition**: The point at which no new information or themes emerge from the data.
    o **Purpose**: Ensures that the data is comprehensive and representative.
    o **Activities**: Continuous data collection and analysis, stopping when saturation is reached.

3. **Validation:**

    o **Definition**: Ensuring that the findings are credible and trustworthy.
    o **Purpose**: Enhances the reliability and validity of the research.

- o **Activities**: Member checking, triangulation, and audit trails.

Importance of Addressing Interpretation Issues

- **Credibility**: Ensures that the findings are credible and trustworthy.
- **Reliability**: Enhances the consistency and reliability of the research.
- **Validity**: Ensures that the findings are valid and applicable to the research context.

Writing Research Reports

Overview

Writing research reports involves presenting the findings of qualitative data analysis in a clear, concise, and compelling manner. Effective reporting ensures that the insights gained from the data are communicated to stakeholders and can inform decision-making.

Key Components of a Research Report

1. **Introduction**:

    - o **Definition**: Provides an overview of the research and its objectives.
    - o **Purpose**: Sets the context and scope of the research.
    - o **Activities**: Introducing the research problem, objectives, and significance.

2. **Literature Review**:

    - o **Definition**: Summarizes existing research on the topic.

- o **Purpose**: Provides a theoretical and empirical context for the study.
- o **Activities**: Reviewing relevant literature, identifying gaps, and situating the study within the broader context.

3. **Methodology**:

- o **Definition**: Describes the methods used to collect and analyze data.
- o **Purpose**: Ensures transparency and replicability.
- o **Activities**: Describing the research design, data collection methods, and analysis techniques.

4. **Results**:

- o **Definition**: Presents the findings of the research.
- o **Purpose**: Communicates the insights gained from the data.
- o **Activities**: Reporting themes, patterns, and theories, supported by data excerpts.

5. **Discussion**:

- o **Definition**: Interprets the results and relates them to the literature.
- o **Purpose**: Provides meaning and context to the findings.
- o **Activities**: Discussing implications, limitations, and future research directions.

6. **Conclusion**:

- o **Definition**: Summarizes the key findings and their significance.

- o **Purpose**: Provides a clear and concise summary of the research.
- o **Activities**: Summarizing the main points, highlighting contributions, and suggesting future work.

Importance of Effective Reporting

- **Communication**: Ensures that the findings are clearly communicated to stakeholders.
- **Impact**: Enhances the impact of the research by informing decision-making.
- **Transparency**: Ensures that the research process is transparent and replicable.

Practical Application of Data Reporting and Analysis

To effectively implement data reporting and analysis, organizations should follow a structured approach. Here are the steps to achieve successful data analysis and reporting:

1. Define Objectives

Start by defining clear, specific objectives for the data analysis. These objectives should align with organizational goals and be measurable and achievable.

2. Collect Data

Gather relevant data using appropriate methods such as surveys, interviews, and automated tools. Ensure that the data is comprehensive and representative.

3. Analyze Data

Apply appropriate data analytic strategies to examine and interpret the data. Use qualitative and quantitative techniques as needed to gain comprehensive insights.

4. Interpret Findings

Interpret the findings carefully, ensuring that interpretations are grounded in the data. Address potential biases and validation issues to ensure credibility and reliability.

5. Write the Report

Present the findings in a clear, concise, and compelling manner. Ensure that the report includes all key components and effectively communicates the insights gained from the data.

6. Communicate Results

Share the report with relevant stakeholders to inform decision-making and drive action. Use presentations, dashboards, and other communication tools to ensure that the findings are understood and acted upon.

7. Continuous Improvement

Adopt a culture of continuous improvement, where data analysis and reporting are regularly reviewed and refined based on performance data and feedback. This ensures that the organization remains agile and responsive to changing needs and market conditions.

Case Studies and Real-World Examples

Example 1: Company A's Data-Driven Decision-Making

Company A, a software development firm, faced challenges with inconsistent quality and frequent defects in their software products. To address these issues, the company initiated a data-driven decision-making program, starting with defining clear objectives and collecting relevant data. They applied descriptive and predictive analytics to examine process performance and identify areas for improvement.

By following a structured approach to data analysis and reporting, Company A achieved significant improvements in their software quality. They saw a reduction in the number of defects, improved user satisfaction, and faster time-to-market for their products. The data-driven decision-making program also fostered a culture of continuous improvement, enabling the organization to adapt to changing needs and market conditions.

Example 2: Company B's Qualitative Insights

Company B, a global IT service provider, sought to improve its software development processes to better meet customer needs and enhance productivity. The company decided to adopt qualitative data analysis techniques, which emphasize understanding user experiences and perceptions.

To implement qualitative analysis, Company B conducted user interviews, focus groups, and usability testing. They applied grounded theory analysis to identify themes and patterns in the data, generating theories grounded in user experiences. The company used these insights to enhance user-centric design and improve overall user satisfaction.

By embracing qualitative data analysis, Company B achieved significant improvements in its software development processes. They saw faster project delivery times, improved software quality, and increased customer satisfaction. The qualitative insights also enhanced the organization's ability to respond to changing requirements and market conditions, fostering a culture of continuous improvement.

Conclusion

Data reporting and analysis are essential tools for understanding, controlling, and improving software development processes. By applying data analytic strategies, conducting qualitative data analysis, using grounded theory analysis, addressing interpretation issues, and writing effective research reports, organizations can transform raw data into actionable insights. Implementing these practices requires commitment, resources, and a willingness to change, but the benefits in terms of enhanced performance, reduced risks, and increased stakeholder satisfaction are substantial. Through practical application and ongoing refinement, organizations can leverage data reporting and analysis to achieve significant advancements in their software development capabilities and overall performance.

CHAPTER 8: SYSTEMS DEVELOPMENT METHODOLOGIES

Introduction

In the dynamic world of software development, choosing the right methodology is crucial for delivering high-quality systems on time and within budget. Systems development methodologies provide structured approaches to managing the complexities of software development, ensuring that projects are executed efficiently and effectively. This chapter explores traditional and alternative systems development methodologies, focusing on the Systems Development Life Cycle (SDLC), its phases, tools and techniques, alternative methodologies, and risk management.

Traditional Systems Development Life Cycle (SDLC)

Overview

The Systems Development Life Cycle (SDLC) is a traditional, structured approach to developing information systems. It provides a framework for planning, designing, implementing, and maintaining systems, ensuring that all necessary steps are taken to deliver a high-quality product.

Phases of SDLC

1. **Planning:**

- Definition: Establishing the project's objectives, scope, and feasibility.
- Purpose: Ensures that the project is aligned with organizational goals and resources.
- Activities: Conducting feasibility studies, defining project scope, and creating a project plan.

2. **Systems Analysis:**

- Definition: Analyzing the current system to identify problems and requirements for the new system.
- Purpose: Provides a clear understanding of the current system and identifies areas for improvement.
- Activities: Gathering requirements, conducting interviews, and creating data flow diagrams.

3. **Systems Design:**

- Definition: Designing the new system based on the requirements gathered during the analysis phase.
- Purpose: Ensures that the new system meets the identified requirements and is efficient and effective.
- Activities: Creating system architecture, designing user interfaces, and developing technical specifications.

4. **Development:**

- Definition: Building the new system based on the design specifications.
- Purpose: Translates the design into a functional system.

- o **Activities**: Writing code, developing databases, and integrating components.

5. **Testing**:

  - o **Definition**: Verifying that the new system meets the specified requirements and performs correctly.
  - o **Purpose**: Ensures that the system is free from defects and meets user expectations.
  - o **Activities**: Conducting unit testing, integration testing, and user acceptance testing.

6. **Implementation**:

  - o **Definition**: Deploying the new system into the production environment.
  - o **Purpose**: Ensures that the system is operational and meets user needs.
  - o **Activities**: Training users, migrating data, and deploying the system.

7. **Maintenance**:

  - o **Definition**: Providing ongoing support and updates to the system.
  - o **Purpose**: Ensures that the system remains operational and meets changing user needs.
  - o **Activities**: Fixing bugs, updating features, and providing user support.

Tools and Techniques in SDLC

1. **Project Management Tools**:

  - o **Definition**: Tools used to plan, track, and manage project activities.

- o **Purpose**: Ensures that the project stays on schedule and within budget.
- o **Examples**: Microsoft Project, Trello, Asana.

2. **Requirements Gathering Tools**:

- o **Definition**: Tools used to collect and document user requirements.
- o **Purpose**: Ensures that the system meets user needs.
- o **Examples**: Surveys, interviews, focus groups.

3. **Design Tools**:

- o **Definition**: Tools used to create system designs and prototypes.
- o **Purpose**: Provides a visual representation of the system.
- o **Examples**: Lucidchart, Visio, Axure.

4. **Development Tools**:

- o **Definition**: Tools used to write and manage code.
- o **Purpose**: Facilitates the development process.
- o **Examples**: Integrated Development Environments (IDEs), version control systems.

5. **Testing Tools**:

- o **Definition**: Tools used to test the system for defects and performance issues.
- o **Purpose**: Ensures that the system is free from defects.
- o **Examples**: Selenium, JUnit, TestNG.

Alternative Methodologies

1. **Prototyping:**

   o **Definition**: Creating a preliminary version of the system to gather user feedback.
   o **Purpose**: Provides a working model to refine requirements and design.
   o **Activities**: Building a prototype, conducting user testing, and refining the design.

2. **Rapid Application Development (RAD):**

   o **Definition**: An iterative development approach that emphasizes rapid prototyping and user involvement.
   o **Purpose**: Delivers functional systems quickly and efficiently.
   o **Activities**: Iterative development, user feedback, and continuous improvement.

3. **Joint Application Development (JAD):**

   o **Definition**: A collaborative approach involving users and developers in the development process.
   o **Purpose**: Ensures that the system meets user needs through active participation.
   o **Activities**: Workshops, collaborative design sessions, and user feedback.

Risk Management in SDLC

Overview

Risk management is a critical component of the SDLC, ensuring that potential risks are identified, assessed, and mitigated throughout the development process.

Key Steps in Risk Management

1. **Risk Identification:**

   o **Definition**: Identifying potential risks that could impact the project.
   o **Purpose**: Ensures that risks are recognized early in the process.
   o **Activities**: Brainstorming sessions, risk checklists, and historical data analysis.

2. **Risk Assessment:**

   o **Definition**: Evaluating the likelihood and impact of identified risks.
   o **Purpose**: Prioritizes risks based on their potential impact.
   o **Activities**: Risk matrices, qualitative and quantitative analysis.

3. **Risk Mitigation:**

   o **Definition**: Developing strategies to reduce the likelihood or impact of risks.
   o **Purpose**: Ensures that risks are managed effectively.
   o **Activities**: Risk response planning, contingency planning, and risk monitoring.

4. **Risk Monitoring:**

   o **Definition**: Continuously monitoring risks to ensure they are managed effectively.
   o **Purpose**: Ensures that risks are addressed promptly.
   o **Activities**: Regular risk reviews, risk dashboards, and reporting.

Importance of Risk Management

- **Early Identification**: Identifies potential issues before they become critical.
- **Proactive Measures**: Allows for proactive measures to mitigate risks.
- **Stakeholder Confidence**: Enhances stakeholder confidence in the project's success.

Practical Application of Systems Development Methodologies

To effectively implement systems development methodologies, organizations should follow a structured approach. Here are the steps to achieve successful system development:

1. Define Project Objectives

Start by defining clear, specific objectives for the project. These objectives should align with organizational goals and be measurable and achievable.

2. Choose the Right Methodology

Select the appropriate methodology based on the project's needs and organizational capabilities. Traditional SDLC is suitable for well-defined projects, while alternative methodologies like RAD and JAD are better for projects requiring rapid development and user involvement.

3. Plan and Prepare

Develop a detailed project plan that outlines the scope, schedule, and resources. Ensure that all stakeholders are aligned and understand their roles and responsibilities.

4. Execute the Plan

Implement the chosen methodology, following the defined phases and activities. Use appropriate tools and techniques to support each phase of the development process.

5. Monitor and Control

Regularly monitor project progress and control risks. Use project management tools to track activities and ensure that the project stays on schedule and within budget.

6. Test and Validate

Conduct thorough testing to ensure that the system meets specified requirements and performs correctly. Validate the system with users to ensure it meets their needs.

7. Implement and Maintain

Deploy the system into the production environment and provide ongoing support and maintenance. Ensure that the system remains operational and meets changing user needs.

8. Continuous Improvement

Adopt a culture of continuous improvement, where processes are regularly reviewed and refined based on performance data and feedback. This ensures that the organization remains agile and responsive to changing needs and market conditions.

Case Studies and Real-World Examples

Example 1: Company A's SDLC Implementation

Company A, a software development firm, faced challenges with inconsistent quality and frequent delays in project delivery. To address these issues, the company adopted the traditional SDLC methodology, starting with a thorough planning phase to define project objectives and scope. They conducted detailed systems analysis to gather requirements and designed the new system based on these requirements.

By following a structured approach to system development, Company A achieved significant improvements in their development processes. They saw a reduction in project cycle times, improved software quality, and increased customer satisfaction. The SDLC implementation also fostered a culture of continuous improvement, enabling the organization to adapt to changing needs and market conditions.

Example 2: Company B's Agile Transformation

Company B, a global IT service provider, sought to improve its software development processes to better meet customer needs and enhance productivity. The company decided to adopt Agile methodologies, which emphasize iterative development, customer collaboration, and continuous improvement.

To implement Agile, Company B conducted training sessions for its development teams, introduced Agile tools and practices, and restructured its project management processes. They also established metrics to measure the impact of Agile adoption, such as cycle time, defect density, and customer satisfaction.

By embracing Agile methodologies, Company B achieved significant improvements in its software development processes. They saw faster project delivery times, improved software quality, and increased customer satisfaction. The Agile transformation also enhanced the organization's ability to respond to changing requirements and market conditions, fostering a culture of continuous improvement.

Conclusion

Systems development methodologies provide structured approaches to managing the complexities of software development, ensuring that projects are executed efficiently and effectively. By understanding and applying traditional and alternative methodologies, organizations can deliver high-quality systems that meet user needs and organizational goals. Implementing these methodologies requires commitment, resources, and a willingness to change, but the benefits in terms of enhanced performance, reduced risks, and increased stakeholder satisfaction are substantial. Through practical application and ongoing refinement, organizations can leverage systems development methodologies to achieve significant advancements in their software development capabilities and overall performance.

CHAPTER 9: RISK MANAGEMENT AND DECISION MAKING

Introduction

In the realm of software development and IT service management, risk management is a critical practice that ensures projects and operations are executed with a clear understanding of potential challenges and their impacts. Effective risk management not only identifies and mitigates risks but also supports informed decision-making, thereby enhancing the likelihood of successful outcomes. This chapter explores the principles and practices of risk management, focusing on risk identification, assessment, treatment, mitigation, and strategic approaches to managing risks.

Introduction to Risk Management

Overview

Risk management is the systematic process of identifying, assessing, and mitigating risks to minimize their potential impact on projects and operations. It involves proactive planning and the development of strategies to handle uncertainties and potential adverse events. Effective risk management is essential for ensuring that projects are completed on time, within budget, and to the satisfaction of stakeholders.

Key Concepts in Risk Management

1. **Risk**: The possibility of an event occurring that could have a negative impact on the project or organization.
2. **Uncertainty**: The lack of complete certainty about the outcome of an event.
3. **Impact**: The effect of a risk event on the project or organization.
4. **Likelihood**: The probability of a risk event occurring.

Importance of Risk Management

- **Proactive Planning**: Helps in identifying potential issues before they become critical.
- **Minimizing Impact**: Reduces the potential negative effects of risks.
- **Stakeholder Confidence**: Enhances confidence in the project's success.
- **Compliance**: Ensures adherence to regulatory and industry standards.

Risk Identification and Assessment

Overview

Risk identification and assessment are the initial steps in the risk management process. These steps involve recognizing potential risks and evaluating their likelihood and impact.

Key Steps in Risk Identification and Assessment

1. **Risk Identification:**

- o **Definition**: The process of identifying potential risks that could impact the project or organization.
- o **Purpose**: Ensures that all potential risks are recognized early in the process.
- o **Activities**: Brainstorming sessions, risk checklists, and historical data analysis.

2. **Risk Assessment:**

- o **Definition**: Evaluating the likelihood and impact of identified risks.
- o **Purpose**: Prioritizes risks based on their potential impact.
- o **Activities**: Risk matrices, qualitative and quantitative analysis.

Tools and Techniques for Risk Identification and Assessment

- **Risk Checklists**: Predefined lists of potential risks based on past experiences and industry standards.
- **SWOT Analysis**: Evaluating strengths, weaknesses, opportunities, and threats.
- **Delphi Technique**: A structured communication technique to reach a consensus among experts.
- **Scenario Analysis**: Developing hypothetical scenarios to understand potential impacts.

Importance of Risk Identification and Assessment

- **Early Detection**: Identifies potential issues before they become critical.
- **Prioritization**: Helps in prioritizing risks based on their potential impact.

- **Resource Allocation**: Ensures that resources are allocated effectively to manage risks.

Risk Treatment and Mitigation

Overview

Risk treatment and mitigation involve developing strategies to reduce the likelihood or impact of identified risks. These strategies aim to manage risks proactively, ensuring that their potential negative effects are minimized.

Key Strategies for Risk Treatment and Mitigation

1. **Risk Avoidance**:

   - **Definition**: Taking steps to avoid the risk altogether.
   - **Purpose**: Eliminates the risk by avoiding the situation that causes it.
   - **Activities**: Changing project scope, avoiding certain technologies.

2. **Risk Reduction**:

   - **Definition**: Reducing the likelihood or impact of the risk.
   - **Purpose**: Lessens the potential negative effects of the risk.
   - **Activities**: Implementing additional controls, conducting regular audits.

3. **Risk Sharing**:

   - **Definition**: Sharing the risk with another party, such as an insurance company or a vendor.

- o **Purpose**: Distributes the risk among multiple parties.
- o **Activities**: Contractual agreements, insurance policies.

4. **Risk Acceptance**:

- o **Definition**: Accepting the risk and preparing for its potential impact.
- o **Purpose**: Acknowledges the risk and prepares for its occurrence.
- o **Activities**: Developing contingency plans, setting aside reserves.

Tools and Techniques for Risk Treatment and Mitigation

- **Risk Response Planning**: Developing detailed plans to address identified risks.
- **Contingency Planning**: Preparing alternative plans in case the risk materializes.
- **Risk Monitoring**: Regularly monitoring risks to ensure they are managed effectively.

Importance of Risk Treatment and Mitigation

- **Proactive Measures**: Allows for proactive measures to manage risks.
- **Minimizing Impact**: Reduces the potential negative effects of risks.
- **Stakeholder Confidence**: Enhances stakeholder confidence in the project's success.

Enterprise Risk Management (ERM)

Overview

Enterprise Risk Management (ERM) is a comprehensive approach to managing risks across the entire organization. It involves identifying, assessing, and mitigating risks at the enterprise level, ensuring that all aspects of the organization are aligned with risk management strategies.

Key Components of ERM

1. **Risk Governance:**

   - **Definition**: The framework for managing risks at the organizational level.
   - **Purpose**: Ensures that risk management is integrated into the organization's governance structure.
   - **Activities**: Establishing risk management policies, defining roles and responsibilities.

2. **Risk Identification and Assessment:**

   - **Definition**: Identifying and evaluating risks across the organization.
   - **Purpose**: Provides a comprehensive view of potential risks.
   - **Activities**: Conducting risk assessments, developing risk profiles.

3. **Risk Treatment and Mitigation:**

   - **Definition**: Developing strategies to manage identified risks.
   - **Purpose**: Ensures that risks are managed effectively.
   - **Activities**: Implementing risk treatment plans, monitoring risk performance.

4. **Risk Monitoring and Reporting:**

- o **Definition**: Continuously monitoring risks and reporting on their status.
- o **Purpose**: Ensures that risks are managed proactively.
- o **Activities**: Regular risk reviews, risk dashboards, and reporting.

Importance of ERM

- **Comprehensive Approach**: Provides a holistic view of risks across the organization.
- **Alignment with Strategy**: Ensures that risk management is aligned with organizational strategy.
- **Enhanced Decision-Making**: Supports informed decision-making by providing a clear understanding of risks.

Strategic Risk Management

Overview

Strategic risk management involves integrating risk management into the organization's strategic planning process. It ensures that risk management is not just a reactive activity but a proactive component of strategic decision-making.

Key Components of Strategic Risk Management

1. **Risk-Adjusted Decision-Making**:

   - o **Definition**: Making decisions that take into account the potential risks and their impacts.
   - o **Purpose**: Ensures that decisions are informed by a clear understanding of risks.

o **Activities**: Risk-adjusted project evaluation, scenario analysis.

2. **Risk Appetite and Tolerance**:

   o **Definition**: The level of risk that the organization is willing to accept.
   o **Purpose**: Guides decision-making by setting boundaries for acceptable risk levels.
   o **Activities**: Defining risk appetite statements, setting risk tolerance levels.

3. **Risk-Informed Strategy**:

   o **Definition**: Developing strategies that are informed by risk assessments.
   o **Purpose**: Ensures that strategies are robust and resilient to potential risks.
   o **Activities**: Risk-informed strategic planning, risk-based scenario planning.

Importance of Strategic Risk Management

- **Proactive Approach**: Encourages a proactive approach to managing risks.
- **Alignment with Goals**: Ensures that risk management is aligned with organizational goals.
- **Enhanced Resilience**: Builds resilience by preparing for potential risks.

Practical Application of Risk Management and Decision Making

To effectively implement risk management and decision-making, organizations should follow a structured approach. Here are the steps to achieve successful risk management:

1. Define Risk Management Objectives

Start by defining clear, specific objectives for risk management. These objectives should align with organizational goals and be measurable and achievable.

2. Identify and Assess Risks

Conduct a thorough risk identification and assessment process to identify potential risks and evaluate their likelihood and impact.

3. Develop Risk Treatment Plans

Create detailed risk treatment plans that outline strategies for managing identified risks. These plans should include specific actions, timelines, and responsible parties.

4. Implement Risk Mitigation Strategies

Implement the identified risk mitigation strategies, ensuring that they are aligned with organizational goals. Use appropriate tools and techniques to support risk management activities.

5. Monitor and Report on Risks

Regularly monitor risks and report on their status to ensure that they are managed effectively. Use risk dashboards and reporting tools to communicate risk information to stakeholders.

6. Continuous Improvement

Adopt a culture of continuous improvement, where risk management processes are regularly reviewed and refined based on performance data and feedback. This ensures that the organization remains agile and responsive to changing needs and market conditions.

Case Studies and Real-World Examples

Example 1: Company A's Risk Management Journey

Company A, a software development firm, faced challenges with inconsistent quality and frequent delays in project delivery. To address these issues, the company initiated a comprehensive risk management program, starting with defining clear risk management objectives and conducting a thorough risk identification and assessment process. They identified several key risks, including scope creep, resource constraints, and technical challenges.

Based on the assessment, Company A developed detailed risk treatment plans that included risk avoidance, reduction, sharing, and acceptance strategies. They implemented risk mitigation strategies, such as changing project scope, implementing additional controls, and developing contingency plans. The company also established a risk monitoring and reporting system to ensure that risks were managed effectively.

By following a structured approach to risk management, Company A achieved significant improvements in their development processes. They saw a reduction in project cycle times, improved software quality, and increased customer satisfaction. The risk management program also fostered a culture of continuous improvement, enabling the organization to adapt to changing needs and market conditions.

Example 2: Company B's Strategic Risk Management

Company B, a global IT service provider, sought to improve its risk management practices to better align with its strategic goals. The company decided to adopt a strategic risk management approach, which emphasizes integrating risk management into the strategic planning process.

To implement strategic risk management, Company B conducted training sessions for its management team, introduced risk-adjusted decision-making tools, and restructured its risk management processes to align with strategic goals. They defined risk appetite statements and set risk tolerance levels to guide decision-making. The company also developed risk-informed strategies that were robust and resilient to potential risks.

By embracing strategic risk management, Company B achieved significant improvements in its risk management practices. They saw faster project delivery times, improved software quality, and increased customer satisfaction. The strategic risk management approach also enhanced the organization's ability to respond to changing requirements and market conditions, fostering a culture of continuous improvement.

Conclusion

Risk management and decision-making are essential practices for ensuring the success of software development and IT service management projects. By understanding and applying risk identification, assessment, treatment, mitigation, and strategic approaches to managing risks, organizations can deliver high-quality systems that meet user needs and organizational goals. Implementing these practices requires commitment, resources, and a willingness to change, but the benefits in terms of enhanced performance, reduced risks, and increased stakeholder satisfaction are substantial. Through practical application and ongoing refinement, organizations can leverage risk management and decision-making to achieve significant advancements in their software development capabilities and overall performance.

CHAPTER 10: ESOURCING CAPABILITY MODEL (ESCM)

Introduction

In today's globalized business environment, sourcing has become a critical component of many organizations' strategies. eSourcing, or electronic sourcing, leverages information technology to streamline and enhance the sourcing process. The eSourcing Capability Model (eSCM) provides a structured framework for organizations to assess and improve their eSourcing capabilities. This chapter explores the eSCM, its components, and how it can be applied to achieve better sourcing outcomes.

The eSourcing Capability Model (eSCM)

Overview

The eSourcing Capability Model (eSCM) is a comprehensive framework designed to help organizations assess and improve their eSourcing capabilities. Developed by the Information Technology Services Qualification Center (ITSqc) at Carnegie Mellon University, the eSCM provides a structured approach to managing the entire sourcing lifecycle, from initiation to completion. The model is applicable to both service providers and client organizations, ensuring that both sides of the sourcing relationship are aligned and capable of delivering high-quality services.

Key Components of eSCM

1. **Sourcing Lifecycle**: The eSCM covers the entire sourcing lifecycle, including analysis, initiation, delivery, and completion phases. This holistic approach ensures that all aspects of the sourcing process are addressed, from initial planning to final transition.

   o **Analysis**: Identifying potential sourcing opportunities and analyzing the organization's business functions and processes.
   o **Initiation**: Preparing for sourced service delivery, including negotiating contracts and designing and deploying services.
   o **Delivery**: Managing the delivery of services to the client, ensuring that service levels are met.
   o **Completion**: Transitioning resources and concluding the engagement, ensuring a smooth handover.

2. **Capability Areas**: The eSCM organizes practices into capability areas, which are grouped into three dimensions: ongoing practices, analysis/initiation practices, and delivery/completion practices. These capability areas provide a structured way to assess and improve specific aspects of the sourcing process.

   o **Ongoing Practices**: Functions that are needed throughout the sourcing lifecycle, such as relationship management and service delivery.
   o **Analysis/Initiation Practices**: Practices concerned with analyzing the organization's needs and preparing for service delivery.

- o **Delivery/Completion Practices**: Practices focused on the delivery of services and the completion of the sourcing engagement.
3. **Capability Levels**: The eSCM defines five capability levels that organizations can achieve, ranging from Level 1 (Initial) to Level 5 (Optimizing). Each level represents a different stage of maturity in the sourcing process.

- o **Level 1: Initial**: Processes are ad hoc and often chaotic.
- o **Level 2: Managed**: Processes are planned and controlled, and projects meet their requirements.
- o **Level 3: Defined**: Processes are well-defined and documented, and the organization has a standard set of processes.
- o **Level 4: Quantitatively Managed**: Processes are measured and controlled based on quantitative data.
- o **Level 5: Optimizing**: The organization focuses on continuous process improvement through innovation and defect prevention.

Benefits of eSCM

- • **Holistic Approach**: The eSCM provides a comprehensive framework that covers the entire sourcing lifecycle, ensuring that all aspects of the process are addressed.
- • **Improved Capabilities**: By following the eSCM, organizations can systematically improve their sourcing capabilities, leading to better service delivery and client satisfaction.

- **Risk Mitigation**: The model helps organizations identify and mitigate risks throughout the sourcing process, reducing the likelihood of project failure.
- **Strategic Alignment**: The eSCM ensures that sourcing activities are aligned with the organization's strategic objectives, leading to more effective and efficient sourcing practices.

Implementation Challenges

- **Complexity**: Implementing the eSCM can be complex, requiring a deep understanding of the framework and its components.
- **Resource Intensive**: The process of assessing and improving sourcing capabilities can be resource-intensive, requiring dedicated time and effort.
- **Cultural Resistance**: Organizations may face resistance from employees who are accustomed to existing sourcing practices.

Practical Application of eSCM

To effectively implement the eSCM, organizations should follow a structured approach that includes the following steps:

1. Assess Current Capabilities

Conduct a thorough assessment of the organization's current sourcing capabilities using the eSCM framework. This involves evaluating practices, processes, and performance against the defined capability levels and areas.

2. Identify Improvement Areas

Based on the assessment, identify specific areas for improvement. This may involve enhancing certain practices, implementing new processes, or improving existing ones.

3. Develop an Improvement Plan

Create a detailed improvement plan that outlines the steps needed to achieve the desired capability levels. This plan should include specific actions, timelines, and responsible parties.

4. Implement Changes

Implement the identified changes, ensuring that they are aligned with the organization's strategic objectives. This may involve training employees, updating processes, and introducing new tools or technologies.

5. Monitor and Measure Progress

Regularly monitor and measure progress using established metrics and performance indicators. This helps ensure that improvements are sustained and that the organization continues to move towards higher capability levels.

6. Continuous Improvement

Adopt a culture of continuous improvement, where sourcing practices are regularly reviewed and refined based on performance data and feedback. This ensures that the organization remains agile and responsive to changing needs and market conditions.

Case Studies and Real-World Examples

Example 1: Company A's eSourcing Journey

Company A, a large financial institution, faced challenges with its outsourcing practices, including inconsistent service levels and frequent disruptions. To address these issues, the company adopted the eSCM framework, conducting a thorough assessment of its current capabilities and identifying key areas for improvement. Based on the assessment, Company A developed a comprehensive improvement plan that included enhancing relationship management practices, improving service delivery processes, and implementing new performance metrics.

By following the eSCM framework, Company A achieved significant improvements in its sourcing capabilities, leading to more consistent service levels, reduced disruptions, and higher client satisfaction. The organization also saw a reduction in overall sourcing costs, as improved processes led to greater efficiency and effectiveness.

Example 2: Company B's eSourcing Transformation

Company B, a healthcare provider, sought to improve its IT outsourcing practices to better support its growing operations. The company adopted the eSCM framework, focusing on enhancing its analysis and initiation practices to better identify and prepare for sourcing opportunities. This involved conducting detailed analyses of the organization's IT needs, negotiating more effective contracts, and implementing robust service delivery processes.

Through the implementation of the eSCM framework, Company B achieved significant improvements in its IT outsourcing capabilities. The organization saw enhanced service delivery, improved client satisfaction, and reduced risks associated with outsourcing. Additionally, Company B was able to better align its sourcing activities with its strategic objectives, leading to more effective and efficient IT operations.

Conclusion

The eSourcing Capability Model (eSCM) provides a structured and comprehensive framework for organizations to assess and improve their eSourcing capabilities. By following the eSCM, organizations can achieve more effective and efficient sourcing practices, leading to better service delivery, reduced risks, and higher client satisfaction. Implementing the eSCM requires a commitment to continuous improvement and a willingness to invest resources in enhancing sourcing processes. Through practical application and ongoing refinement, organizations can leverage the eSCM to achieve significant improvements in their sourcing capabilities and overall performance.

CHAPTER 11: ITIL AND IT SERVICE MANAGEMENT

Introduction

In the realm of information technology, the efficient management of services is crucial for ensuring that technology supports business objectives effectively. IT Service Management (ITSM) is a set of practices and processes designed to deliver high-quality IT services to users. The Information Technology Infrastructure Library (ITIL) is a comprehensive framework that provides best practices for ITSM. This chapter explores the ITIL framework, its components, and how it can be applied to enhance IT service management.

The ITIL Framework

Overview

The Information Technology Infrastructure Library (ITIL) is a widely recognized framework for IT Service Management (ITSM). Developed in the UK in the late 1980s, ITIL has evolved over the years to become a cornerstone of IT service management practices. ITIL provides a structured approach to managing IT services, ensuring that they align with business needs and deliver value to the organization.

Key Components of ITIL

1. **Service Strategy**: This stage focuses on defining the strategy for IT services, including understanding

the business needs, defining service offerings, and setting service management policies.

- o **Service Portfolio Management**: Managing the entire lifecycle of services, from conception to retirement.
- o **Financial Management**: Ensuring that IT services are cost-effective and aligned with budget constraints.
- o **Demand Management**: Understanding and managing the demand for IT services to ensure they meet business needs.

2. **Service Design**: This stage involves designing IT services to meet the defined strategy and business requirements.

- o **Service Catalog Management**: Maintaining a catalog of available IT services and their descriptions.
- o **Service Level Management**: Defining and managing service level agreements (SLAs) to ensure services meet agreed-upon standards.
- o **Capacity Management**: Ensuring that IT services have the capacity to meet current and future demands.
- o **IT Service Continuity Management**: Planning for and managing the continuity of IT services in the event of disruptions.

3. **Service Transition**: This stage focuses on transitioning new or changed services into the production environment.

- o **Change Management**: Controlling and managing changes to IT services to minimize disruption.
- o **Release and Deployment Management**: Planning and managing the release of new or changed services.
- o **Service Asset and Configuration Management**: Managing the assets and configurations of IT services to ensure they are accurately documented and controlled.

4. **Service Operation**: This stage involves the day-to-day management of IT services to ensure they operate efficiently and meet user needs.

- o **Event Management**: Monitoring and managing events to ensure they do not escalate into incidents.
- o **Incident Management**: Managing incidents to minimize their impact on users and services.
- o **Problem Management**: Identifying and resolving the root causes of incidents to prevent recurrence.
- o **Access Management**: Controlling access to IT services to ensure security and compliance.

5. **Continual Service Improvement (CSI)**: This stage focuses on continuously improving IT services based on performance data and feedback.

- o **Service Measurement**: Collecting and analyzing data to measure the performance of IT services.
- o **Service Reporting**: Providing reports on service performance to stakeholders.

- o **Improvement Initiatives**: Implementing initiatives to improve service performance based on data and feedback.

Benefits of ITIL

- **Alignment with Business Goals**: ITIL ensures that IT services are aligned with business objectives, delivering value to the organization.
- **Improved Service Quality**: By following best practices, ITIL helps organizations deliver high-quality IT services that meet user needs.
- **Enhanced Efficiency**: ITIL processes help streamline IT operations, reducing waste and improving efficiency.
- **Risk Management**: ITIL provides tools and practices for managing risks associated with IT services, reducing the likelihood of disruptions.
- **Continuous Improvement**: The CSI stage ensures that IT services are continuously improved based on performance data and feedback.

Implementation Challenges

- **Complexity**: Implementing ITIL can be complex, requiring a deep understanding of the framework and its components.
- **Resource Intensive**: The process of assessing and improving IT services can be resource-intensive, requiring dedicated time and effort.
- **Cultural Resistance**: Organizations may face resistance from employees who are accustomed to existing IT practices.
- **Integration with Existing Processes**: Integrating ITIL practices with existing IT processes can be

challenging, requiring careful planning and coordination.

Practical Application of ITIL

To effectively implement ITIL, organizations should follow a structured approach that includes the following steps:

1. Assess Current IT Practices

Conduct a thorough assessment of the organization's current IT practices using the ITIL framework. This involves evaluating existing processes, practices, and performance against the defined ITIL components and best practices.

2. Identify Improvement Areas

Based on the assessment, identify specific areas for improvement. This may involve enhancing certain practices, implementing new processes, or improving existing ones.

3. Develop an Improvement Plan

Create a detailed improvement plan that outlines the steps needed to achieve the desired ITIL maturity levels. This plan should include specific actions, timelines, and responsible parties.

4. Implement Changes

Implement the identified changes, ensuring that they are aligned with the organization's strategic objectives. This may involve training employees, updating processes, and introducing new tools or technologies.

5. Monitor and Measure Progress

Regularly monitor and measure progress using established metrics and performance indicators. This helps ensure that improvements are sustained and that the organization continues to move towards higher ITIL maturity levels.

6. Continuous Improvement

Adopt a culture of continuous improvement, where IT practices are regularly reviewed and refined based on performance data and feedback. This ensures that the organization remains agile and responsive to changing needs and market conditions.

Case Studies and Real-World Examples

Example 1: Company A's ITIL Journey

Company A, a large pharmaceutical organization, faced challenges with its IT service management, including inconsistent service levels and frequent disruptions. To address these issues, the company adopted the ITIL framework, conducting a thorough assessment of its current IT practices and identifying key areas for improvement. Based on the assessment, Company A developed a comprehensive improvement plan that included enhancing incident management practices, improving service level agreements, and implementing new performance metrics.

By following the ITIL framework, Company A achieved significant improvements in its IT service management capabilities, leading to more consistent service levels, reduced disruptions, and higher user satisfaction. The organization also saw a reduction in overall IT costs, as improved processes led to greater efficiency and effectiveness.

Example 2: Company B's ITIL Transformation

Company B, a global call center, sought to improve its IT service management to better support its growing operations. The company adopted the ITIL framework, focusing on enhancing its service transition practices to better manage the release of new or changed services. This involved implementing robust change management processes, improving release and deployment management, and ensuring accurate service asset and configuration management.

Through the implementation of the ITIL framework, Company B achieved significant improvements in its IT service management capabilities. The organization saw enhanced service delivery, improved user satisfaction, and reduced risks associated with IT service disruptions. Additionally, Company B was able to better align its IT services with its strategic objectives, leading to more effective and efficient IT operations.

Conclusion

The ITIL framework provides a structured and comprehensive approach to IT Service Management, ensuring that IT services are aligned with business needs and deliver value to the organization. By following ITIL, organizations can achieve more effective and efficient IT service management, leading to better service delivery, reduced risks, and higher user satisfaction. Implementing ITIL requires a commitment to continuous improvement and a willingness to invest resources in enhancing IT processes. Through practical application and ongoing refinement, organizations can leverage ITIL to achieve significant improvements in their IT service management capabilities and overall performance.

CHAPTER 12: ISO STANDARDS AND MODELS

Introduction

In the world of software development and IT service management, standards play a crucial role in ensuring consistency, quality, and reliability. The International Organization for Standardization (ISO) provides a wide range of standards that help organizations achieve these goals. This chapter explores the ISO standards relevant to software engineering and IT service management, focusing on how they can be applied to enhance processes and deliver high-quality products and services.

The Role of ISO Standards

Overview

The International Organization for Standardization (ISO) is a global network of national standards institutes that develops and publishes international standards. These standards provide a common framework for organizations to ensure their products, services, and processes meet specific quality, safety, and efficiency criteria. In the context of software engineering and IT service management, ISO standards offer a structured approach to achieving excellence and consistency.

Key ISO Standards for Software Engineering

1. **ISO 9000 Series**: The ISO 9000 series of standards focuses on quality management systems. These

standards provide a framework for organizations to ensure their products and services meet customer and regulatory requirements.

- o **ISO 9001**: This standard specifies the requirements for a quality management system (QMS) and is the most widely recognized standard in the series.
- o **ISO 9004**: This standard provides guidelines for performance improvements in a QMS.
- o **ISO 19011**: This standard provides guidelines for auditing quality management systems.

2. **ISO/IEC 12207**: This standard provides a comprehensive framework for the software lifecycle processes. It defines the processes, activities, and tasks associated with software development, from conception to retirement.

- o **Lifecycle Processes**: The standard covers primary processes (e.g., requirements analysis, design, implementation), supporting processes (e.g., documentation, configuration management), and organizational processes (e.g., project management, quality management).

3. **ISO/IEC 15504 (SPICE)**: The Software Process Improvement and Capability Determination (SPICE) model is a framework for assessing and improving software processes. It provides a structured approach to evaluating process capability and identifying areas for improvement.

- o **Process Assessment**: SPICE helps organizations assess their current processes against defined criteria to determine their capability levels.

- o **Capability Levels**: The model defines six capability levels, ranging from Incomplete (Level 0) to Optimizing (Level 5), providing a clear path for process improvement.

Key ISO Standards for IT Service Management

1. **ISO/IEC 20000**: This standard provides a framework for IT service management, focusing on the delivery and management of IT services. It is closely aligned with the ITIL framework and provides a structured approach to managing IT services.

   - o **Service Management**: The standard covers key aspects of IT service management, including service strategy, service design, service transition, service operation, and continual service improvement.
   - o **Certification**: Organizations can achieve certification to ISO/IEC 20000, demonstrating their commitment to high-quality IT service management.

2. **ISO/IEC 27001**: This standard focuses on information security management systems (ISMS). It provides a framework for establishing, implementing, maintaining, and continually improving an organization's information security management.

   - o **Security Management**: The standard covers key aspects of information security, including risk assessment, security policies, and control objectives.

o **Certification**: Organizations can achieve certification to ISO/IEC 27001, demonstrating their commitment to information security.

Benefits of ISO Standards

- **Quality Assurance**: ISO standards provide a framework for ensuring that products and services meet specific quality criteria, leading to higher customer satisfaction.
- **Process Improvement**: By following ISO standards, organizations can systematically identify and address areas for improvement, leading to more efficient and effective processes.
- **Risk Management**: ISO standards help organizations identify and manage risks associated with their products and services, reducing the likelihood of disruptions.
- **Global Recognition**: Achieving certification to ISO standards can enhance an organization's reputation and marketability, demonstrating their commitment to quality and best practices.
- **Compliance**: ISO standards often align with regulatory requirements, helping organizations ensure compliance with relevant laws and regulations.

Implementation Challenges

- **Complexity**: Implementing ISO standards can be complex, requiring a deep understanding of the standards and their requirements.
- **Resource Intensive**: The process of assessing and improving processes to meet ISO standards can be

resource-intensive, requiring dedicated time and effort.

- **Cultural Resistance**: Organizations may face resistance from employees who are accustomed to existing processes and practices.
- **Integration with Existing Systems**: Integrating ISO standards with existing processes and systems can be challenging, requiring careful planning and coordination.

Practical Application of ISO Standards

To effectively implement ISO standards, organizations should follow a structured approach that includes the following steps:

1. Assess Current Practices

Conduct a thorough assessment of the organization's current practices and processes using the relevant ISO standards. This involves evaluating existing processes, practices, and performance against the defined ISO criteria.

2. Identify Improvement Areas

Based on the assessment, identify specific areas for improvement. This may involve enhancing certain practices, implementing new processes, or improving existing ones.

3. Develop an Improvement Plan

Create a detailed improvement plan that outlines the steps needed to achieve the desired ISO maturity levels. This plan should include specific actions, timelines, and responsible parties.

4. Implement Changes

Implement the identified changes, ensuring that they are aligned with the organization's strategic objectives. This may involve training employees, updating processes, and introducing new tools or technologies.

5. Monitor and Measure Progress

Regularly monitor and measure progress using established metrics and performance indicators. This helps ensure that improvements are sustained and that the organization continues to move towards higher ISO maturity levels.

6. Continuous Improvement

Adopt a culture of continuous improvement, where processes are regularly reviewed and refined based on performance data and feedback. This ensures that the organization remains agile and responsive to changing needs and market conditions.

Case Studies and Real-World Examples

Example 1: Company A's ISO 9001 Journey

Company A, a software development firm, faced challenges with inconsistent quality and frequent defects in their software products. To address these issues, the company adopted the ISO 9001 standard, conducting a thorough assessment of its current quality management practices and identifying key areas for improvement. Based on the assessment, Company A developed a comprehensive improvement plan that included enhancing documentation practices, improving quality control processes, and implementing new performance metrics.

By following the ISO 9001 standard, Company A achieved significant improvements in its quality management capabilities, leading to higher quality software products, reduced defects, and increased customer satisfaction. The organization also saw a reduction in overall development costs, as improved processes led to greater efficiency and effectiveness.

Example 2: Company B's ISO/IEC 20000 Transformation

Company B, a global IT service provider, sought to improve its IT service management to better support its growing operations. The company adopted the ISO/IEC 20000 standard, focusing on enhancing its service transition practices to better manage the release of new or changed services. This involved implementing robust change management processes, improving release and deployment management, and ensuring accurate service asset and configuration management.

Through the implementation of the ISO/IEC 20000 standard, Company B achieved significant improvements in its IT service management capabilities. The organization saw enhanced service delivery, improved user satisfaction, and reduced risks associated with IT service disruptions. Additionally, Company B was able to better align its IT services with its strategic objectives, leading to more effective and efficient IT operations.

Conclusion

ISO standards provide a structured and comprehensive approach to software engineering and IT service management, ensuring that processes are aligned with best practices and deliver high-quality outcomes. By following

ISO standards, organizations can achieve more effective and efficient processes, leading to better product and service delivery, reduced risks, and higher customer satisfaction. Implementing ISO standards requires a commitment to continuous improvement and a willingness to invest resources in enhancing processes. Through practical application and ongoing refinement, organizations can leverage ISO standards to achieve significant improvements in their software engineering and IT service management capabilities and overall performance.

CHAPTER 13: CASE STUDIES AND PRACTICAL APPLICATIONS

Introduction

In the realm of software development and IT service management, real-world experiences offer invaluable insights into the practical application of theoretical concepts. This chapter explores several case studies and implementation examples, highlighting the challenges faced, strategies employed, and outcomes achieved. By examining these real-world scenarios, we can extract valuable lessons and develop best practices that can be applied to future projects.

Real-world Case Studies

Case Study 1: Company A's Agile Transformation

Background: Company A, a mid-sized software development firm, was struggling with long project cycles and frequent delays. Traditional waterfall methodologies were proving inefficient, leading to increased costs and reduced customer satisfaction.

Implementation: Recognizing the need for change, Company A decided to adopt Agile methodologies. They began by training their development teams in Agile practices, including Scrum and Kanban. The company restructured its project management processes to support iterative development, continuous integration, and frequent feedback loops.

Outcome: The Agile transformation led to significant improvements in project delivery times, with an average reduction of 30% in cycle times. Software quality improved, as evidenced by a 25% decrease in defect density. Customer satisfaction increased, with higher Net Promoter Scores (NPS) reflecting improved user experiences.

Lessons Learned:

- **Training and Education**: Investing in comprehensive training for all team members is crucial for successful Agile adoption.
- **Incremental Change**: Implementing Agile practices incrementally, rather than all at once, helps in managing resistance and ensuring smooth transitions.
- **Continuous Improvement**: Embracing a culture of continuous improvement allows for ongoing refinement of processes and practices.

Case Study 2: Company B's DevOps Integration

Background: Company B, a global IT service provider, faced challenges with slow deployment cycles and frequent system outages. The traditional separation of development and operations teams led to silos and inefficiencies.

Implementation: To address these issues, Company B initiated a DevOps integration program. They established cross-functional teams that included both developers and operations personnel. The company adopted continuous integration (CI) and continuous deployment (CD) practices, using tools like Jenkins, Docker, and Kubernetes to streamline workflows.

Outcome: The DevOps integration resulted in a 50% reduction in deployment times and a 70% decrease in system outages. The collaboration between development and operations teams led to improved communication and faster issue resolution.

Lessons Learned:

- **Cross-Functional Teams**: Creating cross-functional teams fosters collaboration and reduces silos.
- **Automation**: Automating CI/CD pipelines significantly improves deployment efficiency and reliability.
- **Monitoring and Feedback**: Implementing robust monitoring and feedback mechanisms helps in identifying and resolving issues promptly.

Implementation Examples

Example 1: Implementing Lean Principles in Software Development

Background: A software development team was facing challenges with excessive waste and inefficiencies in their development process. Traditional project management practices were not addressing these issues effectively.

Implementation: The team decided to implement Lean principles, focusing on eliminating waste, optimizing workflows, and enhancing value delivery. They adopted practices such as value stream mapping, just-in-time (JIT) delivery, and continuous improvement.

Outcome: The implementation of Lean principles led to a 40% reduction in project cycle times and a 35% decrease in non-value-added activities. The team was able to deliver higher quality software with fewer defects.

Lessons Learned:

- **Value Stream Mapping**: Identifying and optimizing value streams helps in eliminating waste and improving efficiency.
- **Continuous Improvement**: Embracing a culture of continuous improvement ensures ongoing refinement of processes.
- **Employee Engagement**: Involving team members in identifying and addressing inefficiencies fosters a sense of ownership and commitment.

Example 2: Enhancing Security through DevSecOps

Background: An IT service provider was facing increasing security threats and vulnerabilities in their software products. Traditional security practices were not keeping pace with evolving threats.

Implementation: The company decided to integrate security into the DevOps pipeline, adopting DevSecOps practices. They implemented automated security testing, code reviews, and vulnerability scanning as part of the CI/CD pipeline.

Outcome: The integration of DevSecOps led to a 60% reduction in security vulnerabilities and a 45% decrease in security-related incidents. The company was able to deliver more secure software products, enhancing customer trust and compliance with regulatory requirements.

Lessons Learned:

- **Integrated Security**: Embedding security practices into the DevOps pipeline ensures that security is addressed throughout the development lifecycle.
- **Automation**: Automating security testing and vulnerability scanning improves efficiency and reduces human error.
- **Collaboration**: Encouraging collaboration between development, operations, and security teams fosters a holistic approach to security.

Lessons Learned

1. **Training and Education**: Investing in comprehensive training for team members is crucial for successful adoption of new methodologies and practices.
2. **Incremental Change**: Implementing changes incrementally helps in managing resistance and ensuring smooth transitions.
3. **Continuous Improvement**: Embracing a culture of continuous improvement allows for ongoing refinement of processes and practices.
4. **Cross-Functional Teams**: Creating cross-functional teams fosters collaboration and reduces silos.
5. **Automation**: Automating workflows and processes significantly improves efficiency and reliability.
6. **Monitoring and Feedback**: Implementing robust monitoring and feedback mechanisms helps in identifying and resolving issues promptly.
7. **Integrated Security**: Embedding security practices into development and operations processes ensures that security is addressed throughout the lifecycle.

8. **Employee Engagement**: Involving team members in identifying and addressing inefficiencies fosters a sense of ownership and commitment.

Best Practices and Recommendations

1. **Adopt Agile and DevOps Practices**: Agile and DevOps methodologies can significantly improve project delivery times and software quality. Invest in training and tools to support these practices.
2. **Implement Lean Principles**: Focus on eliminating waste and optimizing workflows to enhance efficiency and value delivery.
3. **Integrate Security into Development**: Adopt DevSecOps practices to ensure that security is addressed throughout the development lifecycle.
4. **Use Automation Tools**: Automate repetitive tasks and processes to improve efficiency and reduce human error. Tools like Jenkins, Docker, and Kubernetes can streamline workflows.
5. **Foster Collaboration**: Encourage collaboration between development, operations, and security teams to foster a holistic approach to software development and management.
6. **Monitor and Measure Performance**: Implement robust monitoring and performance measurement tools to track progress and identify areas for improvement.
7. **Encourage Continuous Learning**: Promote a culture of continuous learning and improvement, where team members are encouraged to stay updated with the latest practices and technologies.
8. **Engage Stakeholders**: Keep stakeholders informed and involved throughout the project lifecycle to

ensure alignment with business goals and user needs.

Conclusion

Real-world case studies and implementation examples provide valuable insights into the practical application of software development and IT service management methodologies. By examining these scenarios, we can extract lessons learned and develop best practices that can be applied to future projects. Implementing Agile, DevOps, Lean, and DevSecOps practices, fostering collaboration, and embracing continuous improvement are key to achieving successful outcomes. Through practical application and ongoing refinement, organizations can enhance their software development capabilities and overall performance, delivering high-quality products that meet user needs and organizational goals.

CHAPTER 14: FUTURE TRENDS AND CHALLENGES

Introduction

The field of software engineering is in a state of continuous evolution, driven by technological advancements, changing user expectations, and emerging methodologies. As we look to the future, it is essential to understand the emerging trends that will shape the practice of software process improvement and quality management. This chapter explores the future trends in software process improvement, the challenges in implementing quality management, and the broader future directions in software engineering.

Emerging Trends in Software Process Improvement

Artificial Intelligence and Machine Learning

The integration of Artificial Intelligence (AI) and Machine Learning (ML) into software development processes is becoming increasingly prevalent. AI and ML can be used to automate repetitive tasks, predict defects, and optimize workflows. For example, machine learning algorithms can analyze historical data to identify patterns that indicate potential defects, allowing for proactive measures to be taken. AI can also be used to automate code reviews and testing, improving the efficiency and accuracy of these processes.

DevOps and Continuous Integration/Continuous Deployment (CI/CD)

The adoption of DevOps practices and CI/CD pipelines is transforming how software is developed and deployed. By integrating development and operations, organizations can achieve faster deployment cycles, improved reliability, and better collaboration. CI/CD pipelines automate the build, test, and deployment processes, ensuring that changes are quickly and reliably pushed to production. This trend is expected to continue, with more organizations adopting these practices to stay competitive.

Agile and Lean Methodologies

Agile and Lean methodologies continue to gain traction in the software development community. These methodologies emphasize iterative development, customer collaboration, and continuous improvement. Agile practices, such as Scrum and Kanban, help teams respond quickly to changing requirements and deliver value incrementally. Lean principles focus on eliminating waste and optimizing workflows, leading to more efficient and effective processes. The combination of Agile and Lean practices is expected to remain a dominant trend in software development.

Cloud Computing and Microservices Architecture

The shift to cloud computing and microservices architecture is enabling organizations to build and deploy software more efficiently. Cloud platforms provide scalable infrastructure, reducing the need for on-premises hardware and allowing for more flexible resource allocation. Microservices architecture breaks down complex applications into smaller, independent services that can be developed, deployed, and scaled independently. This approach enhances modularity, improves fault isolation, and supports continuous delivery.

Internet of Things (IoT) and Embedded Systems

The growth of the Internet of Things (IoT) and embedded systems is introducing new challenges and opportunities in software development. IoT devices generate vast amounts of data that need to be processed and analyzed in real-time. This requires robust software processes that can handle the complexity and variability of IoT environments. Embedded systems, which are integral to many IoT devices, demand high levels of reliability and performance. As a result, there is an increasing focus on developing software processes that can ensure the quality and security of IoT and embedded systems.

Challenges in Implementing Quality Management

Cultural Resistance

One of the most significant challenges in implementing quality management is overcoming cultural resistance within organizations. Traditional ways of working can be deeply ingrained, making it difficult to adopt new practices and methodologies. Resistance can come from various levels within the organization, from senior management to individual team members. Addressing this challenge requires strong leadership, effective communication, and a clear vision for the benefits of quality management.

Resource Constraints

Implementing quality management practices often requires significant resources, including time, money, and personnel. Organizations may face constraints in allocating these resources, particularly in the face of competing priorities. Ensuring that quality management initiatives receive the necessary support requires careful planning and justification of the benefits.

Integration with Existing Processes

Integrating quality management practices with existing processes can be complex and challenging. Organizations may have established workflows and tools that need to be adapted to support quality management initiatives. This can involve significant changes to how work is done, requiring careful coordination and change management.

Keeping Up with Technological Advancements

The rapid pace of technological change presents a challenge for organizations looking to implement quality management. New tools, techniques, and methodologies are constantly emerging, requiring organizations to stay informed and adapt their practices accordingly. Keeping up with these advancements requires ongoing investment in training and development, as well as a willingness to experiment and innovate.

Measuring and Demonstrating ROI

Demonstrating the return on investment (ROI) of quality management initiatives can be challenging. While the benefits of quality management are often intangible, such as improved customer satisfaction and reduced defects, quantifying these benefits can be difficult. Organizations need to develop robust metrics and reporting mechanisms to measure the impact of quality management practices and demonstrate their value.

Future Directions in Software Engineering

Human-Centric Software Engineering

As software becomes increasingly integrated into our daily lives, there is a growing focus on human-centric software engineering. This approach emphasizes the importance of understanding user needs, behaviors, and experiences in the design and development of software. Human-centric software engineering aims to create software that is intuitive, accessible, and enjoyable to use, enhancing user satisfaction and engagement.

Ethical and Social Implications

The ethical and social implications of software are becoming more prominent as software systems play a larger role in society. Issues such as privacy, security, and algorithmic bias are gaining attention, and there is a growing need for software engineers to consider these implications in their work. Future directions in software engineering will likely include a greater emphasis on ethical design, transparency, and accountability.

Sustainability and Green Software Engineering

With increasing awareness of environmental issues, sustainability is becoming a key consideration in software engineering. Green software engineering focuses on developing software that is energy-efficient, reduces carbon footprint, and promotes sustainable practices. This includes optimizing algorithms to reduce energy consumption, designing software for longevity, and minimizing electronic waste.

Quantum Computing and Software Development

Quantum computing represents a significant leap in computational power, with the potential to revolutionize software development. Quantum algorithms can solve complex problems more efficiently than classical algorithms, opening up new possibilities for optimization, cryptography, and machine learning. As quantum computing becomes more accessible, software engineers will need to develop new skills and methodologies to leverage its capabilities.

Global Collaboration and Distributed Teams

The trend towards global collaboration and distributed teams is expected to continue, driven by advancements in communication technologies and the need for diverse perspectives. Software development teams are increasingly spread across different locations, requiring new tools and practices to support effective collaboration. Future directions in software engineering will likely include a greater emphasis on remote work, virtual collaboration, and cultural awareness.

Conclusion

The future of software process improvement and quality management is shaped by emerging trends, ongoing challenges, and evolving directions in software engineering. By staying informed about these trends and addressing the challenges head-on, organizations can position themselves for success in the rapidly changing landscape of software development. Embracing human-centric design, ethical considerations, sustainability, and new technologies like quantum computing will be crucial for software engineers in the years to come. As we look to the future, the ability to adapt and innovate will be key to delivering high-quality software that meets the needs of users and society as a whole.

APPENDIX A: GLOSSARY OF TERMS

Agile Methodology

Definition: A flexible, iterative approach to software development that emphasizes collaboration, customer feedback, and rapid and flexible response to change. Usage: Agile methodologies, such as Scrum and Kanban, are widely used to improve project delivery times and software quality.

Artificial Intelligence (AI)

Definition: The simulation of human intelligence in machines that are programmed to think like humans and mimic their actions. Usage: AI is increasingly being integrated into software development processes to automate tasks, predict defects, and optimize workflows.

Baseline

Definition: A reference point or standard against which progress is measured. Usage: Establishing a baseline is crucial for tracking improvements in software processes and quality.

Capability Maturity Model Integration (CMMI)

Definition: A process improvement framework that provides organizations with the essential elements of effective processes. Usage: CMMI helps organizations improve their software development processes by providing a structured approach to process maturity.

Cloud Computing

Definition: The delivery of computing services—including servers, storage, databases, networking, software, analytics, and intelligence—over the Internet. Usage: Cloud computing enables scalable infrastructure, reducing the need for on-premises hardware and allowing for more flexible resource allocation.

Continuous Integration (CI)

Definition: A software development practice where developers regularly merge their code changes into a central repository, followed by automated builds and tests. Usage: CI helps ensure that code changes do not break existing functionality and facilitates faster and more reliable software development.

Continuous Deployment (CD)

Definition: A software development practice where code changes are automatically deployed to production without manual intervention. Usage: CD enables organizations to deliver software updates quickly and reliably, enhancing user satisfaction and reducing time-to-market.

DevOps

Definition: A set of practices that combines software development (Dev) and IT operations (Ops) to shorten the systems development life cycle and provide continuous delivery with high software quality. Usage: DevOps fosters collaboration between development and operations teams, leading to faster deployment cycles and improved system reliability.

Enterprise Risk Management (ERM)

Definition: A holistic approach to managing risks across the entire organization, ensuring alignment with strategic objectives and administrative processes. Usage: ERM helps organizations identify, assess, and mitigate risks at the enterprise level, enhancing overall resilience and performance.

Grounded Theory

Definition: A research methodology that involves the systematic collection and analysis of data to develop theories grounded in the data. Usage: Grounded theory is used in qualitative research to identify patterns and generate theories that explain observed phenomena.

Human-Centric Software Engineering

Definition: An approach to software engineering that emphasizes understanding and addressing user needs, behaviors, and experiences. Usage: Human-centric software engineering aims to create software that is intuitive, accessible, and enjoyable to use, enhancing user satisfaction and engagement.

Internet of Things (IoT)

Definition: A network of physical devices embedded with sensors, software, and connectivity to enable the exchange of data. Usage: IoT devices generate vast amounts of data that need to be processed and analyzed in real-time, introducing new challenges and opportunities in software development.

Iterative Development

Definition: A method of software development where the product is developed in small, incremental steps, with each iteration building on the previous one. Usage: Iterative development allows for continuous feedback and refinement, leading to higher quality software that better meets user needs.

Just-In-Time (JIT) Delivery

Definition: A strategy aimed at reducing waste by producing and delivering products only as they are needed. Usage: JIT delivery is a key principle of Lean manufacturing and is applied in software development to optimize workflows and reduce non-value-added activities.

Lean Principles

Definition: A set of principles aimed at minimizing waste and maximizing value in production processes. Usage: Lean principles are applied in software development to eliminate inefficiencies, improve productivity, and enhance quality.

Machine Learning (ML)

Definition: A subset of artificial intelligence that involves the development of algorithms that can learn from and make predictions on data. Usage: ML is used in software development to automate tasks, predict defects, and optimize workflows, improving efficiency and accuracy.

Microservices Architecture

Definition: An architectural style that structures an application as a collection of loosely coupled services, each running in its own process and communicating over a network. Usage: Microservices architecture enhances modularity, improves fault isolation, and supports continuous delivery, making it well-suited for complex applications.

Quality Assurance (QA)

Definition: The process of ensuring that products and services meet specified requirements and are fit for their intended use. Usage: QA involves activities such as planning, inspection, and testing to ensure that software meets quality standards.

Quality Control (QC)

Definition: The process of ensuring that products and services meet specified requirements through inspection and testing. Usage: QC activities include verifying that software meets quality standards, identifying defects, and ensuring that they are corrected.

Risk Appetite

Definition: The level of risk that an organization is willing to accept in pursuit of its objectives. Usage: Defining risk appetite helps organizations make informed decisions about risk management and ensures alignment with strategic goals.

Risk Management

Definition: The process of identifying, assessing, and prioritizing risks to minimize their potential impact on projects and operations. Usage: Effective risk management involves proactive planning and the development of strategies to handle uncertainties and potential adverse events.

Scrum

Definition: An Agile framework for managing and completing complex projects. Usage: Scrum involves iterative development cycles called sprints, regular meetings, and defined roles such as the Scrum Master and Product Owner.

Six Sigma

Definition: A data-driven methodology aimed at improving the quality of processes by identifying and eliminating defects. Usage: Six Sigma uses the DMAIC (Define, Measure, Analyze, Improve, Control) framework to systematically improve process performance.

Software Development Life Cycle (SDLC)

Definition: A structured process for developing software, encompassing planning, design, implementation, testing, deployment, and maintenance. Usage: The SDLC provides a framework for managing the complexities of software development, ensuring that projects are executed efficiently and effectively.

Stakeholder

Definition: Any individual, group, or organization that has an interest or stake in a project or initiative. Usage:

Stakeholders play a crucial role in software development, providing input, feedback, and support throughout the project lifecycle.

User-Centric Design

Definition: An approach to design that focuses on understanding and addressing user needs, behaviors, and experiences. Usage: User-centric design aims to create products that are intuitive, accessible, and enjoyable to use, enhancing user satisfaction and engagement.

Value Stream Mapping

Definition: A visual tool used to document, analyze, and improve the flow of materials and information in a process. Usage: Value stream mapping helps identify and eliminate waste, optimize workflows, and enhance overall process efficiency.

Waterfall Model

Definition: A linear, sequential approach to software development, where each phase of the lifecycle follows the previous one. Usage: The Waterfall model is well-suited for projects with well-defined requirements and minimal changes, providing a structured approach to development.

APPENDIX B: SAMPLE TEMPLATES AND FORMS

Project Plan Template

Project Plan Template

Project   Name: _____
Project   Manager: _____
Start   Date: _____
End Date: _____

---

1. Project Overview

- **Project Description**:
    - o Briefly describe the project's objectives and scope.
- **Project Goals**:
    - o List the specific goals the project aims to achieve.
- **Expected Outcomes**:
    - o Outline the expected results and deliverables.

2. Project Scope

- **In Scope**:
    - o Define what is included in the project.
- **Out of Scope**:
    - o Define what is excluded from the project.

3. Deliverables

- **List of Deliverables**:
    - o Detailed list of all deliverables, including milestones and due dates.

4. Resources

- **Human Resources**:
    - o List team members and their roles.
- **Material Resources**:
    - o List any hardware, software, or other materials needed.
- **Financial Resources**:
    - o Budget allocation for the project.

5. Schedule

- **Milestones**:
    - o Key milestones with dates.
- **Task Breakdown**:
    - o Detailed task list with start and end dates.

6. Risks and Mitigation

- **Risk Identification**:
    - o List potential risks.
- **Risk Mitigation Strategies**:
    - o Strategies to mitigate identified risks.

7. Quality Assurance

- **Quality Standards**:
    - o Standards and guidelines to be followed.
- **Quality Control Measures**:

o   Methods for ensuring quality.

8. Communication Plan

- **Stakeholders**:
    - o   List all stakeholders and their contact information.
- **Communication Channels**:
    - o   Methods and frequency of communication.

9. Approval

- **Project Manager Signature**:

  _____
- **Date**: _____
- **Approval by**: _____
- **Date**: _____

Test Case Template

Test Case Template

Test   Case   ID: _____
Test Case Description: _____

---

1. Test Case Information

- **Test Case Name**:
    - o   Name of the test case.
- **Test Case Objective**:
    - o   Objective of the test case.
- **Test Case Priority**:

o Priority level (High, Medium, Low).

2. Pre-Conditions

- **Pre-Conditions**:
  - o Conditions that must be met before the test case can be executed.

3. Test Steps

- **Step 1**:
  - o Detailed steps to execute the test case.
- **Step 2**:
  - o Continue with additional steps as needed.

4. Expected Results

- **Expected Results**:
  - o Expected outcome of each test step.

5. Actual Results

- **Actual Results**:
  - o Actual outcome of each test step.

6. Status

- **Status**:
  - o Pass/Fail/Blocked.

7. Notes

- **Notes**:
  - o Any additional notes or observations.

Risk Assessment Form

Risk Assessment Form

Project   Name: _____

Assessment Date: _____

1. Risk Identification

- **Risk Description**:
  - o Detailed description of the risk.
- **Risk Category**:
  - o Category of the risk (e.g., Technical, Operational, Financial).

2. Risk Analysis

- **Likelihood**:
  - o Probability of the risk occurring (High, Medium, Low).
- **Impact**:
  - o Severity of the risk if it occurs (High, Medium, Low).

3. Risk Rating

- **Risk Rating**:
  - o Combined rating of likelihood and impact (High, Medium, Low).

4. Risk Mitigation

- **Mitigation Strategy**:
  - o Strategy to mitigate the risk.

- **Responsible Person**:
    - o Person responsible for implementing the mitigation strategy.
- **Due Date**:
    - o Date by which the mitigation strategy should be implemented.

5. Monitoring and Review

- **Monitoring Frequency**:
    - o Frequency of monitoring the risk.
- **Review Date**:
    - o Date for the next review of the risk.

6. Approval

- **Assessor Signature**: _____
- **Date**: _____
- **Approval by**: _____
- **Date**: _____

APPENDIX C: ADDITIONAL RESOURCES

Recommended Reading

1. **"PSP: A Self-Improvement Process for Software Engineers" by Watts S. Humphrey**

   o   A comprehensive guide to the Personal Software Process (PSP), focusing on individual software engineering practices.

2. **"Process Improvement and CMMI® for Systems and Software" by Auerbach Publications**

   o   Offers practical insights into process improvement and the use of CMMI in systems and software development.

3. **"Introduction to Software Process Improvement" by Springer**

   o   An introductory text that covers the basics of software process improvement, suitable for beginners.

4. **"Practical Software Process Improvement" by Artech House**

   o   Provides practical advice and techniques for improving software processes in real-world scenarios.

5. **"Software Engineering (9th Edition)" by Pearson**

- A widely recognized textbook that covers various aspects of software engineering, including process improvement and quality management.

6. **"Six Sigma for Everyone" by George Eckes**

   - An accessible introduction to Six Sigma, a methodology for improving process quality.

7. **"Lean Six Sigma" by Michael L. George**

   - Combines Lean principles with Six Sigma techniques to provide a comprehensive approach to process improvement.

8. **"CMMI: Guidelines for Process Integration and Product Improvement" by SEI**

   - A detailed guide to the Capability Maturity Model Integration (CMMI) framework.

9. **"The Goal: A Process of Ongoing Improvement" by Eliyahu M. Goldratt**

   - A novel that introduces the Theory of Constraints and its application to process improvement.

10. **"Agile Software Development: Principles, Patterns, and Practices" by Robert C. Martin**

    - Focuses on Agile methodologies and their application in software development.

Useful Websites

1. **SEI (Software Engineering Institute)**

   - https://www.sei.cmu.edu/

---

o   The official website of the Software
    Engineering Institute, offering resources and
    information on CMMI and other software
    engineering practices.

2. **ISO (International Organization for
   Standardization)**

   o   https://www.iso.org/
   o   The official website of ISO, providing
       information on international standards,
       including those relevant to software
       engineering.

3. **ITIL (Information Technology Infrastructure
   Library)**

   o   https://www.axelos.com/itil
   o   The official website for ITIL, offering
       resources and certifications related to IT
       service management.

4. **ISTQB (International Software Testing
   Qualifications Board)**

   o   https://www.istqb.org/
   o   The official website for ISTQB, providing
       information on software testing
       certifications and resources.

5. **ProjectManagement.com**

   o   https://www.projectmanagement.com/
   o   A comprehensive resource for project
       management, including tools, templates, and
       best practices.

6. **IEEE (Institute of Electrical and Electronics
   Engineers)**

- o https://www.ieee.org/
- o The official website of IEEE, offering a wealth of resources on software engineering and related standards.

7. **Atlassian (Jira, Confluence)**

- o https://www.atlassian.com/
- o Provides tools and resources for Agile development, project management, and collaboration.

8. **GitHub**

- o https://github.com/
- o A platform for version control and collaboration, widely used in software development.

9. **DevOps Institute**

- o https://devopsinstitute.com/
- o Offers certifications and resources related to DevOps practices.

10. **Lean Enterprise Institute**

- o https://www.lean.org/
- o Provides resources and training on Lean principles and practices.

Tools and Software

1. **Jira**

- o https://www.atlassian.com/software/jira
- o A popular tool for Agile project management and issue tracking.

2. **Confluence**

- https://www.atlassian.com/software/conflue nce
- A collaboration platform for teams to document and share information.

3. **GitHub**

- https://github.com/
- A web-based platform for version control and collaboration, widely used in software development.

4. **GitLab**

- https://about.gitlab.com/
- An integrated DevOps platform that provides tools for the entire software development lifecycle.

5. **Bitbucket**

- https://bitbucket.org/product/
- A web-based version control repository hosting service for source code and development projects.

6. **Selenium**

- https://www.seleniumhq.org/
- An open-source tool for automating web browsers, widely used for testing web applications.

7. **Jenkins**

- https://jenkins.io/
- An open-source automation server that helps automate parts of the software development process.

8. **Docker**

- o https://www.docker.com/
- o A platform for developing, shipping, and running applications in containers.

9. Kubernetes

- o https://kubernetes.io/
- o An open-source platform for managing containerized applications.

10. SonarQube

- o https://www.sonarqube.org/
- o An open-source platform for continuous inspection of code quality.

11. Postman

- o https://www.postman.com/
- o A collaboration platform for API development, including testing and documentation.

12. Trello

- o https://trello.com/
- o A web-based Kanban-style list-making application that helps teams organize and prioritize tasks.

13. Microsoft Project

- o https://www.microsoft.com/en-us/microsoft-365/project/project-management-software
- o A project management tool that helps plan, manage, and track project tasks and resources.

14. Asana

- o https://asana.com/

- o A web and mobile application designed to help teams track their work and manage projects.

15. Lucidchart

- o https://www.lucidchart.com/
- o A web-based diagramming tool that helps teams visualize and collaborate on projects.